S0-AFX-258

# DUTY
# HONOR
# COMPANY

Also by Gil Dorland

*From Idea to Maturity*
*The Business Idea*

# DUTY
# HONOR
# COMPANY

## WEST POINT FUNDAMENTALS
## FOR BUSINESS SUCCESS

### GIL DORLAND
AND
### JOHN DORLAND

HENRY HOLT AND COMPANY ▪ NEW YORK

Copyright © 1992 by Gil Dorland and John Dorland
All rights reserved, including the right to reproduce
this book or portions thereof in any form.
Published by Henry Holt and Company, Inc.,
115 West 18th Street, New York, New York 10011.
Published in Canada by Fitzhenry & Whiteside Limited,
91 Granton Drive, Richmond Hill, Ontario L4B 2N5.

Library of Congress Cataloging-in-Publication Data
Dorland, Gilbert N.
Duty honor company : West Point fundamentals for
business success / Gil Dorland and John Dorland. — 1st ed.
p.    cm.
Includes bibliographical references and index.
1. Success in business.    2. Business ethics.
3. Management—Moral and ethical aspects.
I. Dorland, John.    II. Title.
HF5386.D654    1992
174'.4—dc20                              92-24044
                                              CIP

ISBN 0-8050-2084-5

Henry Holt books are available at special discounts for
bulk purchases for sales promotions,premiums,
fund-raising, or educational use. Special editions or
book excerpts can also be created to specification.
For details contact: Special Sales Director,
Henry Holt and Company, Inc., 115 West 18th Street,
New York, New York 10011.

First Edition—1992

Designed by Victoria Hartman

Printed in the United States of America
Recognizing the importance of preserving the written
word, Henry Holt and Company, Inc., by policy, prints
all of its first editions on acid-free paper.

1   3   5   7   9   10   8   6   4   2

To Colonel Gil,
who epitomizes the best of
a soldier businessman—
and to Lynn, his beautiful bride
of over fifty years.

# CONTENTS

## II. PLANS AND PROCEDURES

## III. DOCTRINES AND TACTICS

## IV. ANNEXES

## V. GLOSSARY OF MILITARY TERMS

# PREFACE

When we entered the gray stone walls of West Point for the first time, all romantic illusions of life as a cadet abruptly vanished. An upperclassman greeted us, shouting commands to line up in squads of ten. "This is your left foot!" he barked. "You will commence all movement on your left foot! Do you understand?"

To be given such an elementary instruction seemed rather demeaning for intellects capable of resolving complex calculus problems. Most of us didn't give much thought to the purpose behind such a demand. But we soon discovered that to start all movement with the left foot wasn't as easy as we had imagined.

The only way that two or more people could march in unison was when each individual started on the same foot. It was that simple. And the continuum of carefully crafted and timed disciplines that were built on this foundation also initially appeared elementary. It was only after we stood back from ourselves that we began to gain the perspective necessary to understand their purposes. In retrospect, it is clear that the "left foot" principle became psychologically ingrained in our minds and crystallized into habit.

In making the transition from Army fatigues to business suits after ten years of military service, we quickly realized that there seemed to be no such singularly defined fundamental as the "left foot" principle in the corporate world. And even years later, after watching on television the execution in Operation Desert Storm of those basic fundamentals of warfare taught at the academy, we were still hard pressed to name one concept in business as meaningful as the "left foot" had been in the military.

This absence of fundamental disciplines inspired us to dust off our old West Point and Army manuals and consider their transferability to business. We do not suggest that their methods and procedures are applicable in their entirety; they are not. We do believe that standardized fundamental guidelines can prevent businesses from straying too far from their critical paths and allow management to focus on the exceptions.

Many of the ideas we uncovered in writing this book appeared at first glance to be common sense. Clearly, military fundamentals have been simplified to be understood by the newest privates and are structured logically and concisely. Although these basic principles may at times seem rather obvious, businesses have frequently ignored their inherent wisdom. It is our hope that our book will help us all refocus on those fundamentals essential for business success.

# ACKNOWLEDGMENTS

We are grateful to Lieutenant General Dave Palmer, the recently retired superintendent of the United States Military Academy at West Point, and the late Major General Chester "Ted" Clifton, Jr. (Retired), for their belief in the book's concept that business can indeed learn from the West Point and military methods, and for sharing their wisdom in the book's shaping and writing. We are most indebted to our father, Colonel Gil Dorland, whose leadership and high ethical standards served as a model for the development of these critical fundamentals throughout the book.

Thanks go to fellow members of the long gray line who have given us the encouragement and support to pursue this endeavor. Particular thanks go to West Point staff, classmates, and friends: Colonel Seth Hudgins, Jr., executive vice president of the Association of Graduates; Bill Raiford, Association of Graduates trustee and highly respected investment counselor; Colonel Peter Stromberg, professor and head of the Department of English; Colonel Tom Karr, director of Military Instruction; and Colonel Will Wilson, director of Academy Advancement, for their perspective of today's West Point, its changes and its future. Thanks also to David Cullum, Colonel USAR (Retired), a true citizen soldier who understands how military principles are applied to the combat zone of business, and to Chris Gillette, who offered a news correspondent's observations of modern weapons and tactics applied in Desert Storm. We are also indebted to Nat Sobel, our agent, for having the vision to perceive the timeliness of such a book in today's new world order.

Finally, a special thanks to Harriet, whose patience, understanding, and support were essential and uplifting throughout the development and writing of this book.

# INTRODUCTION

Early in the autumn of 1991, just a few months before he died, we met with Major General Chester "Ted" Clifton, Jr., who had served as the military aide to President Kennedy and was a highly respected business executive in his own right. Our discussion centered on military fundamentals taught at West Point and their applicability to business. The general, a distinguished graduate of the academy, thought the subject had great merit, and he recalled an anecdote from his years with Kennedy. "How is it that when I ask you to do something," he quoted the president asking him, "or to get the Pentagon to do something, it gets done? Or you come back quickly and tell me why it isn't being done, or even how it is going to be done differently. But when I give one of the cabinet members an order or a directive, first it may never be given any attention whatsoever; and secondly, if it isn't acted upon, I may never hear of it."

Obeying orders had been ingrained in us since our first moment at West Point. Upperclassmen barked commands and followed them with what sounded like a belch: "IRP!" Similar to understanding the left foot principle, it was only later that we learned its meaning: "Immediate Response, Please!" Although immediate response was demanded of us as cadets, it was not the academy's intention that every order be blindly obeyed. Clearly there are situations in the military and in business in

1

which it is more prudent to wait. West Point did, however, prepare us to address promptly each directive when issued, even if the only possible response was that the directive was being reviewed or that action had to be delayed until the timing was right or until all the facts were available.

Years later, having managed and advised businesses that ranged from major corporations to start-up companies, we reflected on the magnitude of changes in the world and noted similar dramatic transformations in the military. For nearly two decades prior to the Gulf War, the military's reputation was plagued by the stigma of Vietnam. The military and its leaders were perceived in degrading stereotypes. All this changed when generals appeared on television in living rooms across the nation and articulated the unfolding strategies of Desert Storm, their language brimming with military terminology and four-syllable words. Except for their camouflage fatigue uniforms, they could have easily passed for top executives in major corporations.

As the war came to an abrupt halt and the diplomats began the political process of settling the drama, we became aware that many of the fundamentals elementary to the tactics and logistics employed on the Kuwaiti battlefield were in continual use in business. Military jargon had even become generic in the world of marketing and finance.

In contemplating these similarities, our book started to take form. We noted how the seven Ps from the academy—"proper prior planning prevents piss poor performance"—proved true in business as in military campaigns. The grim results of Vietnam were an example of the consequences of poor planning by Washington politicians and appointed officials.

The influence of the military on business is not new. The large and complex business organizations of today have borrowed and refined military models developed by the United States forces in World War I and II. In many ways military models laid the foundation for modern business practices. Nonetheless, many contend that military models have little to offer business today. Business is profit motivated and must always attempt to cut unnecessary costs. The military, in contrast, is mission oriented and must spend all its allocated funds within the fiscal year or lose them, and the following year's budget will be reduced accordingly. This fact alone makes for diverse mentalities and discordant methods of achieving goals.

Others contend that the languages of business and the military are incompatible despite the adoption by business of a fair amount of military terminology. The dissimilarity becomes apparent to retiring military personnel attempting to begin a second career in business. The difference between the two cultures results in diverse values, objectives, and mentalities. This is the topic of our discussion in chapter one. These inherent differences, however, neither invalidate nor discount the applicability to business of selected fundamentals taught at West Point.

In a letter written by George Patton on March 6, 1944, to his Third Army subordinates, it is clear that Patton's instructions on how to command are thoroughly valid for business executives. As Colonel Roger Nye, the former Professor of History at the academy, noted in a West Point Newsletter, Patton's letter was "peppered" with the following phrases: "lead in person; visit the front daily; observe, don't meddle; praise is more valuable than blame; make personal reconnaissance; issuing orders is 10%, execution is 90%; plans should be made by people who execute them; tell the troops what they are going to do and what they have done; visit the wounded personally; if you do not enforce discipline, you are potential murderers; do not take counsel of your fears." We should also add: "You can expect only what you inspect."

In relating another anecdote about Kennedy, General Clifton noted that the former president was continually frustrated by the ineptness of reports prepared by his staff. On recalling a format for military orders he had seen while in the Navy, Kennedy instructed the General to find it and to distribute it to his staff members.

General Clifton discovered that the president was referring to a Staff Study instructed at the Army's Command and General Staff College at Fort Leavenworth. The Staff Study and five-paragraph Operations Orders were and still are the basic planning and execution instruments for military operations at all levels of command. They call for the extensive analysis of elements on and off the

3

battlefield that might affect the venture, as well as contingency options to cover conceivable alternatives.

We have modified and successfully used this same format in the preparation of business plans for our own companies as well as international and domestic clients. Translated into business language, this blueprint, from which business ventures are guided, allows for the analysis of a broad spectrum of market, financial, and production information. When processed, they form the basis for premises and assumptions on which financial pro formas and problem-solving and decision-making models can be developed.

The guidelines take into consideration human factors, which always have represented a questionable variable in confronting the future. As the military has experienced, the difference in training, discipline, and leadership between opposing forces has an undeniable effect on performance and outcome. Likewise, business should pay heed to such fundamentals, as have some foreign competitors in their "bottom-up" commitment by the rank-and-file to creating superior quality products.

The West Point leadership method, a total immersion experience, offers concepts intrinsic to the development of leadership traits in business managers. The issue of leadership versus management has been the subject of countless debates. Taking the leadership principles espoused at the academy as a benchmark, it is clear that many executives who perceive themselves as leaders are merely exercising managerial skills, not leadership. There is a distinct gap between managing and leading, as Lester Korn of Korn Ferry International, management recruiters, noted. "The manager," he stated, " keeps everybody in step . . . while the leader decides which way to march and at what pace." Some managers admittedly don't give a damn about their employees. Consequently, many of their best people leave. An entire chapter in this book is devoted to leadership, and throughout the book we touch on this subject and on ethics as well. It is in these two areas that we have found business in general to be most sorely lacking.

West Point encourages competition among its students to promote individual achievement, while strongly encouraging teamwork. "Cooperate and graduate" is a motto shared by most cadets throughout their four years at the academy. This attitude has likewise proven successful in business, perhaps most notably in Japanese companies, which value the inherent benefits of constant cooperation among all departments to achieve quality designs and timely production.

Although the military has responded to advanced technologies and organizational needs by emphasizing more decentralized authority structures, basic tactical maneuvers, such as envelopments and penetrations, have remained relatively unaltered. Similarly, large corporations would benefit from greater flexibility and responsiveness to marketplace changes by placing greater authority at operational levels.

It is not our intent to criticize business unduly or to impose the West Point model inappropriately. Like all institutions of bureaucratic gravity, West Point has its share of imperfections and an "old guard" adverse to change. Yet there are noteworthy attributes to its philosophies and methodologies that we believe are of fundamental value to business in general.

In outlining this book, we decided not to fill the pages with corporate war stories describing how military strategies were employed to capture market shares, such as in the cola and car wars. Nor did we want to illustrate each point with lengthy case histories. Our intent was to write a useful and flexible guide to serve as a reference for the management of business. Although some of the more controversial discussions are aimed at larger institutions, the fundamentals are equally applicable to all businesses, regardless of their size and complexity.

The scope of such an undertaking is so expansive that each chapter could easily be expanded into an entire book. However, because we are from the school that believes ideas should be stated concisely, we have broken the text into three- to five-page discussions covering the military fundamentals that were ingrained in us as young cadets at the academy and their relevancy to the business world.

Because of the broad diversity from chapter to chapter, we have organized the book into five parts. Part one discusses philosophical business concepts, such as leadership, which is strongly influenced by its military model. Part two addresses standardized military procedures and formats, an area in which many businesses fall short. Brief and to the point, these procedures are translated into practical methods for business. Part three examines military tactics and doctrines used in business. Part four provides the reader with a compilation of military procedures and formats all extracted from Army manuals. This may well be the only published commercial book that includes the Army's basic operating documents. Part five defines useful military terminology in easy, understandable terms.

Throughout this book we refer to West Point and Army manuals and quoted pertinent text, formats, and checklists written in plain English. The substitution of civilian counterparts to military terminology should make clear their relevancy to business situations.

The content of the book is not all encompassing. Although our approach may first appear imperious and induce heartburn for those who hold discordant viewpoints, we have nevertheless attempted to address the issues as we see them, which is not necessarily in accordance with consensus opinions espoused by West Point or business and military leaders. We hope that their polemical nature will be provocative enough to provoke further thought.

Critics of the West Point system charge that it suffocates creativity and bold risk taking while rewarding conformity and obedience. They further assert that such limitations are constrictive to business where vision and innovative thinking are essential for commercial success.

With some reservations, we agree that West Point, because of its strict demand for a highly disciplined environment, conditions its students to adhere to specific regulations, SOPs (standing operating procedures), and high standards. Certainly it is true that continual efforts to achieve conformity and adherence to unwavering rules can discourage creative thinking. However, this in no way minimizes the inherent value of the basic tools designed to ensure the successful completion of all kinds of tasks. On the contrary, the perilous consequences of failure on the battlefield compels the military to develop systems and procedures that are "bullet proof" in content and format.

We believe that American businesses have deeply rooted systematic problems and that there has been a growing decline in business leadership and employee work ethics. In order for America's production force to compete and win in the rapidly changing new world order, it first must return to those fundamentals which made it the preeminent global economic power. *Duty, Honor, Company* illustrates how the time-tested military methodologies and standards taught at West Point can effectively assist business management in this endeavor. Like a crisp salute, we have purposely avoided unbridled dialogue in order to accentuate the preciseness of its substance.

# CONCEPTS
# AND
# PHILOSOPHIES

# ·1·

## MILITARY MIND— CORPORATE MIND
### "A Difference in Language"

When we first made the transition from the military into the "real world," the language of business was virtually a foreign language to us. We were like immigrants disembarking a ship on Ellis Island with little understanding of English. We quickly discovered that the skills we had developed in leading soldiers under the severest of stressful conditions were, in the minds of industry, not transferable until we learned to think and communicate in their language.

For decades prior to the Gulf War, the military mind was commonly described in such unsavory terms as regimented, obedient, and dense. The portrait painted was of ineptness and anything but an ideal role model that could be studied by business people. But the precision, coordination, and sound logistics of the coalition air and ground forces displayed in early 1991 demonstrated that there are indeed lessons to be learned from the military for even the most advanced business minds.

The military mind as epitomized by West Point graduates is the result of a system that holds a basic premise that the whole of anything is greater than the sum of its parts. No one is indispensable. The military is a team, a family. To ensure conformity among its vast number of human components, the system is structured with rigid guidelines that are expressed simply in order to be comprehensible to even the lowest level in the hierarchy.

Of course there is no anatomical difference between the brain of a member of the military and a business person. Yet the manner in which they think can be distinctly different. This can be attributed to differences in programming, in language, and in their very "raison d'être."

The ultimate goal of West Point, the traditional source of the Army's leaders, is to prepare its graduates to lead the country in war. Exhaustive training is conducted until individual and collective responses comply with prescribed standards, and those who fail to conform are disciplined.

To mold minds, West Point first strips away one's sense of individuality and background. Psychologically and physically intense, this deprogramming is designed to weed out those who are not capable of the tasks that lie ahead. Anyone who has gone through basic training or boot camp, as it is known in the Marines, can appreciate this arduous ordeal, for they too have undergone a similar metamorphosis in their minds and bodies and have witnessed the evolution of a group ego. Once the mind has been selectively cleansed, the reprogramming process can commence.

Starting with the left foot principle, inch-by-inch reprogramming constructs a cerebral circuitry that functions on a path of logic conducive to reliable performance under the stress of combat. In order to be able to confront successfully the ever-changing dynamics of the battlefield, basic fundamentals of war are instilled in the mind to produce instinctive responses. Such reflexive action often bypasses the intellect, which in urgent situations has no time to ponder and analyze. Essential to the reprogramming process is the maintenance of absolute honesty and ethical behavior at all times, principles that West Point cadets are inculcated with from their very first day at the academy.

It is this basic mental programming that sets the stage for the system to convince young men and women from all walks of life to risk their lives for the reward of a badge, a small strip of ribbon and the ideals they represent. Acknowledging the strong motivational power of such rewards, Napoleon declared that if he had enough ribbon, he could conquer the world. Military minds are trained to be moved by rewards uncommon to business, which takes as its primary goal the making of money.

In order to mold leaders who will respond reliably in combat, the West Point system disciplines cadets to analyze fully all aspects of any operation prior to entering the battlefield. Standardized checklists, formats, and procedures provide a uniform, systematic method that allows commanders to concentrate on the mission and ensures a unified effort by all members of the team involved.

Some critics have charged that the effect of this Spartan discipline on creativity is stifling. Acknowledging that this assessment does have some validity, West Point embarked upon a five-year project in 1986 to address this and other major concerns. The final report, titled "2002—and Beyond: A Road Map to Our Third Century," led to the articulation of academy goals. One of the five outcome goals states: "provide the nation graduates who have a foundation of knowledge in the sciences and humanities, an understanding of various methods of inquiry, the ability to communicate clearly, creativity, intellectual curiosity, and a commitment to continuing intellectual growth."

Lieutenant General Dave Palmer, superintendent of the Military Academy during this period, amplified on this position, noting that

the military leader must strike a balance between disciplined thinking and creative thought. West Point's concern for fostering creativity and developing bold risk takers implies that there will be occasions when the book will be wrong, when following instructions unhesitantly would be the very opposite of professional behavior. But one can not proceed from a premise that indiscipline somehow leads to creativity. Equally unacceptable, clearly, are blind obedience masquerading as disciplined thinking and a disorganized mind posing as an innovative one. Creativity itself is the creature of a rather highly refined and disciplined mental process. Creative commanders through the ages have been disciplined thinkers and hard, leaders mentally able to conceive of alternative actions and with the strength of character to act boldly on their conceptions. Intelligence is required to recognize the right course; moral courage is required to pursue that course even if it is not the safe or easy way. In short, character is the bridge between disciplined thinking and creative action. And West Point's very purpose, remember, is to develop leaders of character.

Whereas innovation has been essential to the development of small entrepreneurial organizations, larger bureaucratic corporations, like the military, tend to discourage creative thinking. Similarly, the corporate mind has been cynically stereotyped in such unflattering terms as ruthless, greedy, and deceitful. Although these charges are in most cases as inaccurate and far-fetched as those leveled at the military, it is true that many corporations, especially those that are publicly owned, have functioned myopically, sacrificing long-term interests for short-term gains.

When we first entered into corporate America, we initially found ourselves seduced by remarks that we were "new blood," exactly what the company wanted. We were different from the management trainees recently recruited from B-school. But from the very first day on the job, we confronted demands from middle management to conform to the company mold and to adopt a company loyalty that discouraged individuality. As we soon discovered, they didn't really want "new blood." Just as the military had required reprogramming of our minds to meet its demands, the corporate world demanded that the mental slate we had developed in the Army be washed clean, and once again we were subjected to a reprogramming process. Looking around at the company managers, we understood that the corporate mind was no different from the military in its need to control.

Unlike the military, where employment had been virtually guaranteed, until the recent build-down, in corporations the fear of termination is constant, and we saw many a corporate lieutenant fretting over it. Fear, we realized, was a major source of motivation. And it was fear that caused behavior that later would prove to be imprudent responses to short-term financial pressures. In many cases, adherence to standardized planning and decision-making guidelines like those used in the military would have caused

14

greater attention to details and resulted in a much less haphazard outcome.

A distressing lack of promptness was pervasive as well. Meetings often commenced well after their scheduled time for reasons we found inexcusable. Appointments were all too frequently delayed or canceled. Our minds had been trained to be synchronized, to be attentive to the exact coordination of events. The infantry crossed the line of departure precisely when the artillery lifted. Delay in action would allow the enemy to regroup, and the potential result was nothing short of disaster.

Certainly the military, with its strict methodology, and the business world, with its creative inclinations, have much to gain and learn from each other.

# · 2 ·

# MANUALS
## "The Bibles"

Early in the 1960s we had the occasion to meet with Bernard Fall, a French scholar and the author of two important books analyzing the communist insurgency movement in South Vietnam. At this time America had only a handful of military advisors in that country, and as young lieutenants, we were open to any and all enlightened opinions on the struggle. Fall asserted that Vietnamese hamlet and village chiefs in the countryside were being assassinated at an alarming rate and replaced by Hanoi-trained cadre. He maintained that the State Department refused to recognize South Vietnam was at war because soldiers weren't being killed. It was quite clear to him then that the Communists were following Mao Tse-tung's seven steps on guerrilla warfare, and that they were already into the second and third phases. It was just a matter of time before the nation's infrastructure would become subject to Hanoi's control and overt hostile actions would commence.

This encounter with Bernard Fall so impressed us that we have recalled it many times over the intervening years. The formula for the insurgent movement and the eventual collapse of Western influence in the region had been recorded in print since 1938, over two decades prior to America's involvement in Vietnam. There were no secrets. The blueprint was available for anyone to see. Yet Fall told us that his warnings fell on deaf ears in Washington.

Similarly, America's enemies do not have to resort to drastic espionage activities to predict how America is likely to respond under most combat situations. Decision-making methods, strategies, and tactics have been in unclassified print for years. Had Saddam Hussein heeded FM 100-5, the Army's two-hundred-page operations manual, he might have foreseen the envelopment that caught him by surprise.

FM 100-5 is the Army's "keystone warfighting manual." As is stated in the preface, the manual "explains how Army forces plan and conduct campaigns, major operations, battles, and engagements in conjunction with other services and allied forces. . . . It presents a stable body of operational and tactical principles rooted in actual military experience and capable of providing a long-term foundation for the development of more transitory tactics, techniques, and procedures." Reading FM 100-5 allows one to climb into the heads of the American military and to see exactly how the armed forces might act and react under most situations and circumstances.

At the conclusion of World War II, a number of senior German generals were debriefed on America's conduct of the war, with particular attention to the operations doctrine as outlined in the manual in use at that time. Based on the valid points of their criticism, revisions were made to the manual. Several editions later, this very manual formed the basis for the Allied operations in Desert Storm.

Equally important to FM 100-5 is FM 101-5, the Army's field manual *Staff Organization and Operations.* Commonly known in the military as the "staff bible," this eight by ten, one-inch-thick reference text prescribes basic guidelines for commanders and their staff to carry out their duties. The manual provides checklists to reduce the probability of inadequate and erroneous plans and orders. There is nothing magical about the procedures detailed in FM 101-5; they are based on common sense, are concise, logical, and expressed in language simple enough to be understood by practically anyone within the system.

FM 101-5's predecessor, *Field Service Regulations,* dates back to 1905, when the American Army began making its first attempts to standardize methodologies. Although there were no firm rules and procedures then, it set the stage for a formal guide to the preparation and planning of war. For example, it recommended a sequence of information gathering as follows: "(1) the enemy or own troops in the vicinity, (2) intentions of the commanding officer, (3) orders for baggage trains and ammunition columns, and (4) location of commander and place for delivery of messages." In 1940 the Army published the first edition of FM 101-5. It was used in World War II and revised in 1950 based on new methods and techniques developed during the Big War. Its current edition remains similar to the 1950 edition despite today's high-tech capabilities.

There are fundamentals common to both business and war, and in fact, some people would say business *is* war. The only differences are the rules by which they are conducted and the severity of consequences. Some veterans of business battles equate financial casualties with those inflicted by bullets and shrapnel. Innumerable heart attack, cancer, and ulcer victims, not to mention bankruptcies and prolonged unemployment, attest to the potential lethality and destructiveness of business combat. In its working manuals, the military has set forth procedures and strategies that can be invaluable in business warfare.

If, indeed, business is war, it is only logical that the procedures and techniques outlined in the Army's manuals apply as well to business planning and decision making. Of course the executive and the commander don't always share the same terminology, but both face the same challenge: to compete against enemies for a stated objective, be it a hill or market share.

# ·3·

# MISSION
## "Raison d'être"

"You will enter the continent of Europe and, in conjunction with other Allied Nations, undertake operations aimed at the heart of Germany and the destruction of her Armed Forces." With this brief directive, one of the world's most enormous and historic missions was given to General Dwight Eisenhower, Supreme Commander of the Allied forces in Europe during World War II. Rarely has an assignment been so ominous and crucial: the future freedom of the world depended on its success or failure.

As defined by the military, the mission is "the task together with the purpose, which clearly indicates the action to be taken and the reason therefor." At West Point and in the military in general, training, duties, and life itself revolve around the concept that the mission is foremost and must be accomplished. There is no excuse for failure, especially in light of the task, which is no less than the defense of the nation. Total concentration is devoted to the mission and the time and effort spent on ancillary activities must be kept to a minimum. Essential to success is the ability to analyze and understand assignments, to transform them into definable and achievable objectives, and to develop and act on plans to accomplish the desired results.

A statement of the mission prefaces all military orders and plans, eliminating any speculation as to what is required. Upon entering West Point, all cadets are promptly instructed that the mission is

19

one's raison d'être. It soon becomes second nature to focus on what is to be accomplished before initiating any action.

In accordance with the concept of chain of command, subordinate units in the military, down to the lowest element, are assigned missions that complement the mission of their superior. The following example excerpted from a U.S. Army Infantry School map exercise in Egypt illustrates how a mission statement becomes more detailed and specific as it flows down from the higher corps command to the subordinate division.

### Higher headquarters (corps) mission:

1st Corps prepares to move to secure SUEZ Canal from PORT TAUFIQ (coordinates VU6012) to BLUE STONE Lake (VU5257) at H-hour, D-day. Be prepared to conduct operations west to CAIRO.

### Next subordinate unit (division) mission:

101st Airborne Division moves H-hour, D-day; screens 1st Corps south flank; conducts airmobile operations to secure terrain; secures ferry crossing site at SUEZ Canal to secure SUEZ Canal vicinity (coordinates VU5825); prepares to initiate offensive operations to the west on order.

Just as the military finds a well-defined statement of mission indispensable to its success, businesses will benefit enormously by developing their own statement of mission or purpose. Properly composed, the statement reflects the organization's values, focus, and long-term visions. It defines the company's niche and goals in a broad but well-articulated manner, providing management with a beacon to hold course and avoid costly distractions. The written expression of a company's direction will help not only managers and employees, but the company's customers and the community it serves, to understand what the company does, what is needed to achieve its goals, and how it will affect the surrounding environment.

To compose a mission statement, businesses can benefit from a technique used by the military to analyze philosophical and factual notions about the company and its purpose. The questions to be addressed should include:

1. What does the company do?
2. What is the area and sphere of the company's operations?
3. What are the company's strengths and weaknesses?
4. What is the acceptable level of risk for the company?
5. What is the level of corporate responsibility of the company?
6. How does the company view its customers?
7. What degree of focus is placed on maximizing the company's value and shareholders' profits?
8. Can the purpose be defined in terms that can be measured?

Once these questions have been answered, a statement can be formulated to reflect the overall long-term purpose of an organization.

A statement formulated for a financial services company addressed the issues of customer, employee, and community concerns. The statement read as follows:

> To meet the full financial needs of profitable retail customer segments and expand increasingly into commercial segments through sound, progressive, and innovative management. Products and services will be provided in a manner to enhance personal service and the company's market position, growth and financial strengths, while contributing to employee relations and the civic betterment of the communities in which the company's offices are located.

Implicit in the statement were the bottom-line implications for shareholders. As is true in the military, subordinate units within the company should be assigned or develop complementary missions that reflect their roles in the overall corporate purpose. The following example illustrates the adherence to mission hierarchy by a retail banking subsidiary of the financial services organization mentioned above.

> Retail Banking is committed to excellence in performance and service. This statement expresses the standards on which each Retail Banking staff member can base their business actions.
>
> Serving our customers is the most important aspect of our job. Providing quality innovative commercial and retail financial services with a high level of personal attention and a constant awareness of the needs of our market is the foundation of our customer service strategy. Retail Banking has adopted the concept of relationship banking based on actively determining our customers' financial needs and matching these needs with the company's services and products. We believe in today's banking world a commitment to a sales and service culture is the key to success. It is understood that sales is, in fact, the ultimate delivery of service to our customers. We want our customers' total banking relationship and do not hesitate to ask for it because we sincerely believe that no other provider of financial services can serve these needs as well as us.

Throughout our careers, in the military and in business, we have observed conflicting requirements arising from an incongruity between the mission and one of its components, the objective. Missions are often compromised by intermediary goals that are narrow in scope and offer only short-term results. Winning the battle, we have learned, does not necessarily mean winning the war. Had Eisenhower reduced the intensity of the Allied offensive after taking the Normandy objectives, the mission of destroying the German war machine would not have been accomplished. Similarly, businesses have lost market advantages by cutting R & D funds, closing vital installations, and reducing marketing budgets in order to achieve short-term financial goals.

To avoid potential confusion between mission and objectives, the military differentiates the two. The mission is an overall statement of purpose, whereas objectives normally consist of a physical object to be taken or defended to help accomplish the mission, such as the Normandy beachheads. Business objectives, on the other hand, usually relate to financial goals, such as annual and quarterly earnings' reports and market shares.

Although we advocate coming to a clear understanding of the mission, it is also true that an excessive preoccupation with mission accomplishment can lead to tunnel vision. Failure to recognize peripheral considerations that at first glance may appear to be inconsequential can hinder the exploration of alternatives that might prove important to the accomplishment of the mission.

# ·4·

# LEADERSHIP VERSUS MANAGEMENT
## "An Immersion Experience"

The first shock to hit us on entering the corporate world was its regimented structure. It was as though we had merely changed uniforms. Perhaps even more shocking was the realization that no one seemed to give a damn about us as individuals once we had joined the company.

Not surprisingly, we felt somewhat out of place, having come from Vietnam, where we had commanded hundreds of men under the most stressful conditions. Gone was the power and prestige of rank, and suddenly the day's activities consisted of little more than pushing typewritten documents from the in-box to the out-box. The vocabulary we had learned in B-school—academic terms concerning theories in micro-economics, econometrics, and simulation models—was hardly the language used in day-to-day business operations. We were dismayed as well to see that as adept at budgeting, marketing, and production many managers appeared to be, few had the slightest clue about how to lead. Naïvely, we assumed this deficiency was limited to middle management and that we would find senior executives demonstrating the leadership qualities that had been ingrained in us at the academy and in the service. However, much to our concern we soon discovered that this lack of leadership permeated all levels of management.

In Beast Barracks, the grueling first summer at the academy, the plebes undergo an endless repetition of drill exercises. During one long and arduous session, we witnessed the difference between the art of leadership and the mechanics of management, concepts that up until then held little meaning for us. An older cadet instructor commanded us to complete a variety of maneuvers commencing with the left foot. Our exhausted bodies slovenly went through the motions as our minds dreamed of being anywhere but there. This continued for weeks until the instructor was replaced by another upperclassman. In no time at all, energy surged into our limbs. In unison, all ten of us in the squad snapped to attention and marched as a single body. The man had ignited in us not only confidence but an almost compulsive need to do our very best.

We were too young to analyze why the two men elicited such different responses from us. Their technical skills were equal. But somehow the second instructor had managed to project his desires and enthusiasm into us so that they became our own. He instilled in us purpose, direction, and motivation.

Countless books and papers have been written on the subject of leadership. But leadership cannot be developed solely from a book or in a classroom. Whether you look upon leadership as an art or a skill, one thing remains clear: it can be learned. Self-awareness, study, training, and most important, experience are vital to the learning process. As General Dwight Eisenhower put it, "the one quality that can be developed by studious reflection and practice is the leadership of men." By studying and applying the fundamentals of leadership for many years in his early life as a cadet and officer, Eisenhower built a vast reservoir of knowledge, experience, and confidence that brought him success in his eventual roles as supreme commander of the Allied forces in Europe and president of the United States.

West Point emphasizes an experiential approach to the development of leadership as it works to achieve its purpose of "providing the Nation with leaders of character who serve the common defense." As noted in the academy's catalog: "Everything that cadets experience during their time at West Point is aimed at developing leaders of character." Cadets are immersed in a Spartan environment, a four-year human laboratory designed to nurture on a daily basis leadership traits that enable its graduates to lead men under the extreme pressures of combat.

The immersion process presents a series of increasingly demanding leadership situations, challenging cadets to develop people skills. It begins with the role of a follower, which is succeeded by intermediary roles of increased responsibility to direct and motivate peers and underclassmen, and it culminates four years later in the leadership of the entire corps of four thousand cadets. Unlike most universities, at West Point all activities outside the academic classroom are under the supervision of cadet leaders, placing a weighty duty upon them very early in their lives. While the demand for excellence is high, the officer cadre monitoring the cadets recognize that an essential part of the learning process is making mistakes. To build leadership skills, the cadets must be permitted to make their own decisions, right or wrong.

Accompanying this development process is an evaluation system to measure the progress and deficiencies of each individual. The evaluations are not limited to superiors rating subordinates, but include ratings by peers and, under certain conditions, by subordinates rating superiors.

In the early stages of the leadership development program, plebes today are taught eleven leadership principles to help guide them in the forming of their own individual styles and techniques. These principles, as discussed in the Army's FM 22-100, *Military Leadership,* are entirely suitable for integration in business.

## Principles of Leadership

1. *Know yourself and seek self-improvement.* Identify your strengths and weaknesses. Set goals for each weakness or desired improvement. Develop plans to achieve goals. Evaluate progress toward goals.
2. *Be technically and tactically proficient.* Be knowledgeable in all aspects of your job. Be able to pass this on to your fellow workers.
3. *Seek responsibility and take responsibility for your actions.* When you see a problem, initiate actions to solve it. Do not wait on others to tell you to do it or say "it's not my job." If

you have made a mistake, admit your errors, accept criticism, and promptly correct the matter.

4. *Make sound and timely decisions.* Use problem-solving, decision-making, and planning methods to come to a rapid assessment of the situation and make the most appropriate decision. Indecisiveness causes confusion and lack of confidence and could result in fatal consequences.

5. *Set the example.* As a role model, this is your most important leadership skill. You should not ask your subordinates to do anything you would not do yourself. As a leader, you should earn the respect of your subordinates, not demand it.

6. *Know your soldiers and look out for their well-being.* Take the time to learn about your people by listening to them. Know what it takes to motivate each individual; it will probably vary. It is important to recognize their need to be needed. If you take care of your troops, they will take care of you.

7. *Keep your soldiers informed.* Don't just give orders; explain the rationale for the orders. An informed organization considers itself to be a part of the effort, not just going through the motions because it was told to. Your personnel cannot continue to grow and perform if you keep them in the dark.

8. *Develop a sense of responsibility in your subordinates.* Delegation of responsibilities will enhance the development of subordinates. It will reflect your confidence in them and cause them to seek additional responsibilities. Acknowledging their accomplishments fosters their initiative.

9. *Ensure that the task is understood, supervised, and accomplished.* Orders and directives should be clearly understood and all personnel need to know what is expected of them. There is a thin line between undersupervision and oversupervision. Giving the order is ten percent; the other ninety percent is making sure it gets done.

10. *Train your soldiers as a team.* Teamwork occurs when all members of the team are proficient in their respective assignments and have the mutual respect and trust of each other. A team must have its own spirit and confidence in its

ability to accomplish its mission. *Cohesion builds confidence, morale, courage and will to fight in the individual.*
11. *Employ your unit in accordance with its capabilities.* You must have a clear understanding of your unit's capabilities and limitations. Focus on essential goals. Inform your superiors of serious limitations. Do not lower standards and expectations.

Like many of the principles presented in this book, these ideas consist of common sense stated in simple terms. Each has its own merits and complements the other ten. These fundamentals are not axioms to be deliberated over or ignored when they might seem inconvenient. They are a way of life.

Principle five, "set the example," is one of the leadership characteristics most often overlooked by business. It can separate true leaders from mere managers. In combat, military leaders dig their own foxholes. They eat after their men have been served. They demand from subordinates only what they are prepared to do themselves. Leaders, even four-star generals, visit their troops in the field. A simple handshake accompanied by a simple comment—"damn good job"—can have a dramatic, positive effect on the esprit de corps. Similar minor considerations can make huge differences in subordinates' performances in corporations as well.

In business, the distance between top executives and factory workers can be vast. Executives are often insulated from the human elements of the business and enjoy special perks and privileges. Of course it would be unrealistic to expect every executive of a major corporation to visit every cubicle within the organization. Still, executives can make efforts to create a work environment that engenders a sense of self-esteem within the employees, which in turn can result in higher morale and product quality. Most top executives need to make efforts to visit their "troops," and to let the workers know they are important. Management by Wandering Around (MBWA) goes a long way toward boosting morale and performance.

Drawing on the total immersion method used at West Point, we have outlined points for consideration in forming a program to develop leadership skills in business managers. This eight-point list provides concepts for tailoring an appropriate course of action. The program is not intended to be limited to management trainees, but is useful for people operating at all levels of responsibility. It is particularly effective when employed in this manner, since often the greatest leadership offenders are those executives entrenched in the we've-always-done-it-that-way syndrome.

## Leadership Immersion Process

1. A formalized program should be directed, reviewed, and personally endorsed by the CEO. The first meeting should be introduced by CEO, with subsequent informal sessions to discuss progress, provide encouragement, and validate management's continuing endorsement of the program.

2. An initial formal classroom instruction should discuss the basic principles of leadership and their relevant applications in the business environment. Classroom study should continue on a periodic basis to familiarize all participants with basic skills and introduce new techniques.

3. Early in the program, if possible, participants should be taken to a site away from the office or physical plant. Under unfamiliar surroundings, small groups are formed and placed in stressful situations that require cooperative efforts to complete specific tasks. Immersion in such activities without the benefit of directives from above and artificial support systems demands leadership skills and techniques to confront problems successfully. Although some groups may be less capable than others, the experience should prove helpful in developing confidence and communication skills in the workplace.

4. Conduct on-the-job training and evaluation with clear feedback on progress and shortcomings. Evaluations are to be based on performance objectives discussed prior to the commencement of the program.

5. Expose participants to progressively more difficult decision-making situations with commensurate authority. They should not be told how to make decisions, nor should

improper decisions be immediately counteracted. When mistakes are made, participants should be counseled with constructive criticism and not intimidation.

6. Individual advancement in the chain of command should be based on the capacity for and demonstrated performance of leadership.

7. Managers should be given the opportunity to change positions and disciplines periodically within the organization. This will broaden their vision and overall understanding of the business. New environments will demand the application of leadership skills in order to earn the respect of unfamiliar subordinates.

8. Successful participants should be encouraged to accept added responsibilities. Those who do not meet expectations should be given additional training and, if necessary, reassigned to positions that do not demand leadership qualities.

In its various forms, the immersion process has become more widely accepted by business and educational institutions who believe that today's managers need better leadership skills. They recognize that academic and work environments tend to restrict vision and fail to instill the confidence required to make sound decisions in a rapidly changing world. Even traditional B-schools, such as Wharton, have revamped their curricula, shifting the emphasis from building elaborate abstract models to developing leadership skills for the real world of global competition, commencing with an intensive "outward bound" course. Another method of leadership development involves the creation by senior managers of work environments that foster innovative ideas. In such an atmosphere, subordinates are encouraged to think beyond the immediate and to build their visionary capability, an essential yet often neglected leadership trait.

E. M. Estes, former president of General Motors, well summarized our philosophy of leadership when he stated: "Leadership is the courage to admit mistakes, the vision to welcome change, the enthusiasm to motivate others, and the confidence to stay out of step when everyone else is marching to the wrong tune."

# ·5·

# HONOR—ETHICS
## "Merely a Perspective?"

Honor may be perceived as an anachronism, lost long ago along with chivalry and other idyllic notions. Imagine a world in which a person's word was as powerful as reams of legal documents, and a simple handshake signified an irrevocable commitment. The return of such conditions today would eliminate the pervasive need for lawyers.

Obviously, today's environment is not so ideal, presenting daily conditions where money is the prime motivation. Ironically, veterans who experienced the real bullets of military wars tend to be defenseless in the business world, where money is the prime motivator. Similarly, we found ourselves somewhat naïve in the face of the manipulative words of less than truthful people upon first encountering them in business. We had assumed that everyone lived according to the same principles we had learned in the military. West Point had ingrained in us that "a cadet will not lie, cheat or steal, nor tolerate those who do." The Code is absolutely clear. There are no degrees of right and wrong. A lie is a lie; cheating is cheating; stealing is stealing, regardless of the magnitude and circumstances.

Some maintain that it would be absurd to impose these standards on society at large. Veracity is a matter of perspective, they contend, and one person's truth can be another person's lie. Opposing viewpoints is what litigation is all about.

Quickly we learned that in order to protect ourselves we first had to "qualify" those with whom we conducted business. The size of a person's office or the cut of his suit was no reflection of his intentions or honesty. Having observed trusted bankers, politicians, and even religious leaders—the pillars of our communities—suddenly exposed as dishonest, we began to doubt the moral fiber of America, to witness a negative influence on how American business was conducted, and to wonder whether ethical fundamentals, as we knew them, were valid in today's society.

In combat, an unconditional adherence to integrity is absolutely essential to survive the most demanding situations. There are no contracts between individuals to guarantee their flanks will be covered as they assault enemy positions. In the heat of battle there may be nothing more than a nod of the head—a silent indication of a commitment and the recognition that the consequences of failing to fulfill that commitment could be the death of comrades. Under such conditions, there is no place for lies or for reneging on one's word.

Upon entering West Point, we were issued the *Bugle Notes,* a compact handbook for incoming plebes. The dedication at the beginning of the book states that the "traditions held sacred by the members of the Long Gray Line are herein compiled; they are your heritage. Cherish them, and pass them on to those who will follow after you." Seven pages discussing the subject of honor are prefaced by a statement written in 1920 by Secretary of War Newton D. Baker, who summarized why an exact code of ethics was mandatory for the military.

> Men may be inexact or even untruthful, in ordinary matters, and suffer as a consequence only the disesteem of their associates, or even the inconvenience of unfavorable litigation, but the inexact or untruthful soldier trifles with the lives of his fellowmen, and the honor of his government; and it is, therefore, no matter of idle pride but rather of stern disciplinary necessity that makes West Point require of her students a character of trustworthiness which knows no evasions. In the final analysis of the West Point product, character is the most precious component.

We learned at the academy that the Code had no geographical boundaries or limits. It applied at all times, whether we were in or out of uniform. As young plebes, we were constantly aware of the need to live and act by the Code. At first it was rather intimidating. One slip could mean expulsion from the academy. Many of us came from less than ideal environments and naturally had on occasion done what was necessary to survive. But now there was no survival outside the parameters of the Code.

Following the ethical directive of the Cadet Prayer, "to choose the harder right instead of the easier wrong, and never to be content with the half truth when the whole can be won," the academy complements the Code with three basic Rules of Thumb. These are rules of fairness that anyone can use in evaluating the ethicality of their intentions.

1. Does this action attempt to deceive anyone or allow anyone to be deceived?
2. Does this action gain or allow the gain of a privilege or advantage to which I or someone else would not otherwise be entitled?
3. Would I be satisfied by the outcome if I were on the receiving end of the action?

Unfortunately, the military strayed from these rules during the Vietnam conflict. Defense Secretary Robert McNamara's free-enterprise management, not unlike those in place in many modern corporations, espoused "ticket punching" as the track to early promotion and "body counts" as the bottom line. At the expense of the unit as a whole—and of the subordinates within these units—primary emphasis was placed upon individual success. Personal achievement too often overshadowed integrity and ethical fundamentals. As is true of many of the corporate models, the entire system suffered. By the early 1970s, discipline had eroded, morale had deteriorated, and the American military had lost credibility at home and globally.

After years of introspection, military leaders recognized that a divergence from basic fundamentals had occurred and instigated a return to the principles that once made it a highly effective fighting force. The Army understood that "anyone can be ethical when there are no pressures to be unethical." Military leaders concluded as well that "self-interest is probably the most common cause of unethical acts." Responding to these findings, they developed rules of conduct to assist commanders in dealing with various "ethical dilemmas."

Morality and ethics are viewed by many in the business world with skepticism. The environment of almost total distrust is not only reflected in the public exposure of scandals and schemes, but in the pervasive willingness to do whatever is necessary to make a buck. Devoid of a sense of personal ethics, individuals can succumb to an uncontrollable desire to accumulate personal wealth and power. Pressured by organizational demands, they are driven to commit immoral acts. Throughout the business world, we found companies that were motivated by the promise of short-term profits, with management more intent than ever on impressing the analysts and stockholders, regardless of ethical considerations. Equally disconcerting is a blatant indifference to misconduct, which results in the development of a culture that fosters even greater improprieties.

Large segments of our nation appear to be infected by this blasé attitude, and resistance is sporadic at best. In most instances, it is not until a major scandal occurs that the hue and cry of the public arises, followed by a demand for a cleanup. Wall Street, S & L, banking, insurance, real estate, religious, and political chicaneries are clear examples of a widespread lack of ethical conduct within our society.

Responding to this deterioration in ethical standards, many companies and professional organizations have established their own codes of conduct. Their guidelines serve as a notice that individual misconduct will not be tolerated—and that ignorance is not an acceptable excuse. Tailored to meet specific company needs, these policies become a standard for individual conduct and are often required to be acknowledged in writing. Minimally, a code of business ethics should include considerations such as the following:

Your company's reputation for integrity is its most valuable asset and is determined by the conduct of its directors, officers, and employees. Each of us must manage our personal and business affairs to avoid situations that might lead to a conflict or even suspicion of a conflict between self-interest and duty to the company, its customers, and its shareholders. One's company position must never be used, directly or indirectly, for private gain, to advance personal interests, or to obtain favors or benefits for oneself, a member of one's family, or any other person.

The following provides guidance for the exercise of personal judgment in avoiding conflicts of interest or the appearance of such conflicts.

*Confidential Information:* No information with respect to the affairs of the company or any of its customers should be used by any officer or employee for his or her own benefit. Similarly, no such information should be disclosed to any outsider so that someone else can obtain a benefit.

*Personal Investment—Outside Business:* No officer or employee should engage in any outside business activities which will interfere with his duties at the company, divide his loyalty, or allow a possibility of conflict of interest. Outside employment is not permitted without prior written approval. Officers and employees must make full disclosure if he or his family has a substantial ownership or beneficial interest in firms that are suppliers, purchasers, or competitors of the company.

*Acceptance of Gifts or Entertainment:* No officer or employee should accept a substantial gift or excessive entertainment from any customer, supplier, or any person or firm seeking favor or business from the company.

If any officer or employee has knowledge of any violations of these principles, he should report the pertinent facts in writing to the CEO.

Regardless of the stated ethical standards, such a program can only be effective with the complete endorsement and practice by all members of senior management, beginning at the top with the CEO. This support cannot be merely in the form of lip-service, but must be visibly practiced and supported in daily activities and managerial decisions. An attitude that says "do what I say, not what I do" will be quickly discerned by the employees, and any attempts to create an ethical environment will seem a blatant hypocrisy. Senior managers must continually set the example, display an open and demonstrative intolerance for unethical acts, and reinforce and reward those who have the courage to stand up and point out improprieties. In addition to fostering a positive and respectable work climate, such a program should prove to be an effective "early warning system," exposing subterfuge or misconduct before they become corporate crises. This is more effective than "damage control" measures after the fire has broken out. Finally, management should review its own demands on its organization and responses to outside pressures to ensure that their employees are not being subjected to requirements or rewarded for results that can only be achieved by unethical actions or questionable methods.

It is not our intent to preach or to impose West Point's stringent standards where they are not welcome. Honor and ethics, like religion, are matters of personal conscience. However, we do believe that greed and an excessive pressure to succeed have contributed to a decline in the moral principles that allow humankind, individually and collectively, to live in harmony with oneself and one's neighbors. Thus we contend that we should be mindful of West Point's three Rules of Thumb, simple as they may appear, as we conduct our business and daily lives.

# ·6·

# DISCIPLINE
## "A Way of Life"

For eleven long months, as West Point plebes, we kept our chins pressed to our gullets, chests raised high, backs rigidly straight, and gaze unwaveringly directed straight ahead. This posture was maintained even at the dining table, as we sat on the forward edge of the chair and maneuvered bite-sized morsels of food on our utensils first vertically up and then horizontally toward our tightly opened mouths, all the while keeping our heads erect and our eyes fixed on the plate in front of us. This we perceived to be discipline.

Years later the pain of this ordeal—known as bracing—is far from forgotten. Although officially bracing was said to be done in order to teach us to "develop a correct posture" by insisting we adopt an exaggerated position of military attention, it had degenerated into a way for upperclassmen to haze plebes. Discipline had become analogous with punishment, restraint, and control, and it was clear that bracing provided certain cadets of a tyrannical bent with a legal means to abuse other people of lower status.

In our remaining three years at the academy, we were caught in a vexing dilemma over the true meaning and purpose of discipline. Having been subjected to its narrowly accepted definition as "punishment meant to correct," it was only after graduating that we began to see its positive aspect as a means to elicit a specific pattern of behavior or character. The draconic practices that existed when we were cadets were eventually seen as archaic and fortunately have since been prohibited. But we learned something from the sadistic upperclassmen who had taken such pleasure in harassing us as plebes: how not to administer discipline effectively. Ironically, their concept of discipline contradicted the long-standing definition given by Major General John Scholfield, former superintendent of West Point, in his landmark 1879 address to the Corps of Cadets:

> The discipline which makes the soldiers of a free country reliable in battle is not to be gained by harsh or tyrannical treatment. On the contrary, such treatment is far more likely to destroy than make an army. It is possible to impart instructions and give commands in such a manner and such a tone of voice to inspire in the soldier no feeling but an intense desire to obey, while the opposite manner and tone of voice cannot fail to excite strong resentment and a desire to disobey. The one mode or the other of dealing with subordinates springs from a corresponding spirit in the breast of the commander. He who feels the respect which is due to others cannot fail to inspire in them regard for himself, while he who feels, and have manifested disrespect toward others, especially his inferiors, cannot fail to inspire hatred against himself.

Discipline, on a personal basis, means developing a mind-set that adheres to the practice of proper prior planning, attention to detail, and punctuality. It is what enables individuals and groups to perform to the best of their abilities regardless of mental stress, physical exhaustion, or distractions.

The military, in FM 22-100, considers an organization disciplined when "the unit is orderly, obedient, controlled, and dependable . . . and does its duty promptly and effectively in response to orders, or even in the absence of orders." The commander is the underlying force that builds discipline within an organization. He sets and communicates the standards, draws the lines of tolerance, and administers disciplinary actions to offenders. Some use fear as a prime motivator; others use the offer of incentives. Ideally all commanders, regardless of their individual techniques, should set an example.

In order to gauge the level of discipline within a unit, the military developed eight indicators. Like many of its checklists, this list of indicators is uncomplicated and leaves a broad latitude for interpretation.

- All missions are accomplished.
- Soldiers have confidence and a sharp appearance.
- Soldiers are proud of their unit; they know it has a good reputation.
- Weapons and equipment are well maintained.
- Soldiers at all levels are actively engaged in doing their duties. They do not waste time.
- Soldiers cooperate; they willingly help one another.
- Training is well planned, well conducted, and thoroughly evaluated for individual and unit strengths and weaknesses.
- The unit fights successfully under stress.

An experienced eye can detect the measure of discipline within a unit by merely observing something as simple as a soldier's hand salute. A sharp, crisp greeting reflects personal and organizational pride and a positive feeling that proclaims confidence, professionalism, and a "can-do" approach to all tasks. From this utterly routine gesture, his entire unit's morale, combat readiness, and leadership can be surmised without setting foot on its premises.

Discipline within the context of business can be more difficult to measure. Typically, the term conjures the image of a tightly run company with "no-nonsense" bosses at the helm. An undisciplined company, by contrast, is considered disorderly, vacillating, and lethargic, and as having little or no direction or purpose. Foreign competitors are often stereotyped as being rigidly controlled; the Germans and the Japanese are most often so categorized.

There are many interpretations of what constitutes discipline, but the most pragmatic method of assessing it is to look at results. Such subtleties as a salesperson's courtesy and thoughtfulness or the manner in which a secretary answers phone calls can reveal more about organizational behavioral patterns than observation of a member of senior management who stands in the spotlight. Similarly, the timeliness of reports, adherence to prescribed procedures, and promptness in starting meetings are sure indications of a company's basic character and of the direct involvement of senior management at all levels.

The discipline instilled in us as West Point cadets was accomplished by drastic measures. Although such an approach is, needless to say, unfit for business, positive and meaningful discipline is an integral, essential part of an individual's and organization's ability to perform. As is true of most fundamentals, the establishment and maintenance of discipline must emanate from the top. Executives and management alike can benefit greatly by taking into consideration the following military guidelines extracted from its leadership manual in developing their own procedures.

1. Ensure that norms which contribute to discipline are established and strengthened.
2. Set high, yet realistic, standards in all things that relate to the success of your unit.
3. Communicate those standards clearly.
4. Ensure that those standards which are critical to the organization are understood and attained.
5. When standards are not met, analyze the situation and decide on a course of action for handling the situation. Ask the following questions:

   • Did the troops know what was expected?
   • Was it communicated clearly and effectively?
   • Did they know how to do what was expected?
   • Did they have the capability to do it (time, stamina, knowledge, skills, authority)?
   • Did they deliberately fail to meet the standards (laziness, unpleasant duty, anger directed at supervisor)?

Many free thinkers and self-styled entrepreneurs may take a contrary viewpoint to any kind of formalized discipline, feeling that it restricts their style and creativity. Notwithstanding the desire for individual freedom, there is an undeniable truth to the words of Vince Lombardi, who was an assistant football coach at West Point from 1949 to 1953 and said, "I've never known a man worth his salt who in the long run, deep down in his heart, didn't appreciate the grind, the discipline. There is something in good men that yearns for discipline."

# · 7 ·

# ORGANIZATIONAL STRUCTURE
## "Who's the Boss?"

At West Point, we were instructed on theories of chain of command, span of control, unity of command, and formal and informal lines of communication. Upon graduating, we were each assigned a six-digit number and thrust into our first assignments, which were mapped out in a vast bureaucratic latticework of boxes and lines much like the one we had been taught to work within at the academy. As is customary for many new second lieutenants, the assignment we both were given was near the lowest rung in the command hierarchy: we were to serve as platoon leaders of forty enlisted men. The infantry platoon had a set structure, explicitly prescribed by the Department of Army's "Table of Organization and Equipment (T O & E)."

The Army developed the T O & E to establish the number, grade, and skills of personnel authorized for each unit throughout the entire system. An objective template, it is designed so that units can function effectively regardless of which individuals occupy the slots. With the T O & E in place, there is never any question as to who is in charge, which is critical in combat situations where personnel are replaced at rapid rates because of casualties. Rigidly enforced, these standards remove all structuring options from the commanders, with the exception of special units in certain authorized cases. In these exceptions, there remains a commitment to the laws of span of control and the fluid flow of communication, up and down and sideways, among all levels within the command.

Organizational structuring was present even in ancient armies. However, it wasn't until the industrial revolution, when businesses ballooned into unmanageable sizes, that such structuring fundamentals were adopted by commercial enterprises. Today they are an integral aspect of most businesses.

Upon entering a new client's company, one of our first requests is to see a map of the organization. Sometimes executives of small companies pride themselves on not having one, claiming that it would inhibit creativity. At most companies, however, the executive will unfold elaborate diagrams displaying boxes upon boxes, stacked in varying orders and connected by straight lines. Printed inside the boxes are job titles, names, and specific responsibilities. Like medical X rays, the charts illustrate areas of potential problems and stress. For example, they reveal where excessive numbers of subordinates report directly to one superior, or where subordinates have more than one boss. They also give evidence of potential role distortions and unclear lines of communication. The stressed faces of employees one sees on taking a walk through a company confirm these initial diagnoses.

When we first entered into the corporate world, we encountered a bureaucratic structure not unlike the Army's. Initially, we unquestioningly accepted it as being both necessary and wise and attempted to fit into the roles assigned to our positions. But as we developed a fluency in the language of business, it became clear that some people wanted to discourage us from voicing opinions. Boxes on the chart became filters that screened what we perceived as innovative concepts that would be beneficial to the company as a whole. The particular configuration of boxes allowed managers to lord over their fiefdoms and to threaten to shorten the careers of subordinates who crossed the invisible lines separating their territory from that of other managers. This proprietary mentality clogged the communication pipeline, particularly when the line ran from the bottom up. Slowly, as though a little spigot had been turned, our stomachs began to churn with acid, and our youthful ambitions were taken over by stress.

Stress caused by an improperly designed work structure can disable an organization, limiting its performance in terms of both quality and quantity. Over a lengthy period of time, this kind of organizational stress can cause dysfunctional behavior, fatigue, and possible breakdown. By rearranging the structure, however, it can easily be corrected. Conversely, stress arising from poor leadership, fear and uncertainty, and demands that exceed capability, is more difficult to alleviate.

Numerous techniques have been developed over the years to cope with organizational stress, ranging from centralized to decentralized and autocratic to more liberal forms of control. Some believe that an organization should be designed to fit the strengths of individual personalities. Others suggest that the function of an organization should determine its structure and that people should be assigned certain jobs based on their ability to fill the specific requirements of the position. Ultimately, there is no one solution; each situation demands its own particular approach. Regardless of the tactic, it is essential to clarify from the outset who is boss and to define responsibilities and levels of authority.

The organizational map—as unprogressive as it sometimes can appear to be—is a surefire way to remove doubt about who's the boss and who reports to whom. It must, however, be properly configured; matrix structures that assign two or more bosses authority over the same subordinates and resources inevitably create multiple chains of command with a potential for conflicting priorities and demands. More often than not, matrix organizations result in unbridled frustration and organizational stress.

To minimize the anxiety that is created when there are too many chiefs, when a subordinate is responsible for activities outside the jurisdiction of his or her immediate superior, all directives should be given to the immediate superior to pass along to the subordinate in order to avoid confusion. Similarly, to prevent staff members from circumventing the formal network and making demands on subordinates as though they hold equal authority with the line manager, the staff should be instructed to route their communications through the superior, unless an alternate arrangement has been explicitly approved by a higher authority. Likewise, committees must respect the chain of command; seldom have we seen a situation where a committee is assigned the role of decision maker. The single box standing at the apex of a hierarchical pyramid in a company's organizational map should leave no question that this is where the buck stops.

# ·8·

# UNIFORMS
## "Walking Résumés"

At civilian cocktail parties and office meetings, much attention is focused on individual careers, income levels, and social status. In the military, most of this information can be surmised from the ornaments an individual wears on his uniform. The uniform, in fact, is like a walking résumé. At West Point, we learned that by simple observation of certain details on a person's uniform, an enormous amount of specific and useful data was yielded without a single word of conversation ever being exchanged. Among the telling details are:

- *Name tag.* This eliminates the necessity of memorizing names, which can be especially burdensome in large organizations.
- *Symbol of rank.* You immediately understand the "pecking order" and how much money they make.
- *Branch of service insignia.* This indicates basically what type of job a person holds. It also helps to differentiate the warriors from rear-echelon administrators.
- *Ribbons.* A quick résumé of achievements and tours of duty, with special emphasis on those involving warfare. Ribbons commending valor in combat are placed at the top and are arranged in a descending order of level of commendation.

These are perhaps the most valued statement on the "résuméd" uniform.

- *Crests.* Appearing on epaulets, crests specify the unit to which one is assigned, i.e., regiment or command.
- *Unit patch.* Appearing on the left shoulder, this patch designates the major organization in which one is currently serving.
- *Combat patch.* Appearing on the right shoulder, this patch designates the unit to which one was assigned during war and the type of unit, and indicates the type of job performed.
- *Overseas bars.* These denote how long one served in a war zone.
- *Qualification badges.* These badges designate special qualifications and skills such as pilot, parachutist, rifle marksman, and the level of expertise or experience.
- *Hat/beret.* These indicate the type of special unit to which one belongs, such as ranger, airborne, or special forces.

Few people realize that military uniforms have been in common use only since the seventeenth century. Regardless of how they might be portrayed in spectacular movies and on television, uniforms of the Middle Ages consisted primarily of body protection, shields, and weapons. Knights on crusades to the holy lands displayed individuality in their garments, and the remainder of their armies dressed in civilian clothing. It was not until 1792 that the United States Congress required military commanders to clad their regiments uniformly at their own expense, with commanders often selecting the styles and colors. Only after the Civil War was there a concentrated effort to standardize military attire. In accordance with the fashion of the time, several styles appeared from the late 1800s on. The West Point cadet gray uniform is one of the few that has not markedly changed over the years.

Since they were first designed, military uniforms have consistently been of two types: one for dress and the other for field work. However, much to our consternation, work fatigues and combat boots became less clearly distinguished from dress attire. We can well recall hours spent fastidiously spit shining the toes

47

and heels of combat boots designed to be worn when slogging through mud and dirt and the irritation of the pliable cotton fabric of fatigues that were starched to tuxedo shirt stiffness.

As commanders, we sought to strike a balance between appearance and utility. Naturally, this became even more difficult when we were sent, as part of the first wave of United States combat units, to Vietnam. After a few months in the jungles, the troops began to look like a ragtag confederate army. Our leather boots and cotton fatigues rotted apart, and it became imperative for us to get boots and fatigues that could withstand the tropical environment. No longer did spit and polish and parade-worthy impeccability prevail.

Nonetheless, when extraordinary circumstances do not preclude it, there needs to be an orderliness in one's dress, whether in the sweltering heat of the Asian jungles, the windswept Arabian deserts, the offices of corporate America, or the shops of small businesses. A clean, well-groomed personal appearance is a good indicator of pride and discipline within an individual and organization. But the gleam of fine leather shoes or the cost of a person's suit should not be the deciding factor of an individual's promotion rating.

Uniforms should enhance, not hinder, performance. In this regard, the practicality of some civilian uniforms seems dubious. The businessman's tie, for example, is perplexing. It is uncomfortable and feels as though it restricts the flow of blood to one's brain. We are victims of this age-old tradition, and ties are a mandatory item of dress in many circles. Spurred on by a thriving fashion industry that continually changes its styles, sizes, fabrics, and colors—and that has inflated its price outrageously—the tie is unlikely to disappear any time soon. Although it can seem terribly constrictive, the tie is nevertheless a symbol of respectability and responsibility. And as is true in the military, one must acknowledge current social expectations and accept its definition of appropriateness in matters of dress. In a sense, failure to wear a tie, or wearing an inappropriate color or style of tie, can be as detrimental to accomplishing a task as wearing inadequate fatigues and boots that fall apart in the line of duty.

Like the military, businesses have their own uniforms. A business person's attire often gives a first impression that turns out to be lasting. It not only puts the wearer into a particular frame of mind, but creates a certain psychological effect on one's colleagues. An individual's profession and position can often be immediately deduced from the style and color of his or her clothing.

Bankers and accountants traditionally wear dark suits, white shirts, and moderate ties to project an image of stability and conservatism. Attorneys often wear three-piece suits with a gold key chain and Phi Beta Kappa medallion draped between vest pockets to cast an image of intellectual prowess. Stockbrokers, aiming to impress others with their investment successes, typically adorn themselves with expensive monogrammed silk shirts, diamond studded cuff links, hand-painted ties, and Rolex watches. At one time IBM employees were distinguished by their dark blue suits and crisp white cotton shirts. Many corporate employees wear on their lapels a pin commemorating years of faithful service as part of their uniform. These are but a few examples and may vary from region to region. The uniforms worn by members of different professions and organizations, although not as obvious as the military uniform, in effect function the same: as a walking résumé.

# ·9·

# HEROISM—CHARACTER
## "Human Trait Shrouded in Mystery"

A mere smell, sound, or a wispy shadow can trigger the replay of an indelible scene in one's distant past. Vietnam remains vividly alive in the memories of most of us who fought there, and in particular, the faces of a few special men who gave their lives in those war-torn jungles.

One young man, now dead for twenty some years, was among the courageous heroes we had the honor of knowing. Only eighteen years of age, he was too young to drink or even vote in many states but old enough to be drafted into the Army to fight for his country. As is true of most young men and women at his age, there was nothing about him that clearly showed he would go on to perform an exceptionally gallant act. And yet one dark night when we heard the thud of a Vietcong grenade landing in the mud in our command post, before any of us could react, this young man had thrown his body on the destructive ball of steel.

Why did he and others like him instinctively sacrifice their lives? Was it environmental conditioning? Was it something specific in their upbringing? Were they just plain crazy?

Volumes of psychological studies have speculated on what motivates some to act bravely and risk their lives in combat and in other perilous circumstances. There are no courses at West Point or at any institution that teach people how to be a hero; there are no guidelines on how to exhibit extraordinary courage when faced with life-threatening circumstances. In short, one of the most admirable human traits remains shrouded in mystery.

In combat, commanders learn to anticipate the varying capabilities of their men to function under severe stress. They know that some will freeze while others will perform laudably. They further understand that intelligence and willingness to conform are not the criteria for heroic or cowardly actions. Nor are age, race, religion, physical prowess, or social and economic background. In the heat of battle even the toughest athletes may crumble when confronted with death, while the skinny bookworm may respond with remarkable valor.

Heroic acts are often the result of an instinctive reaction to fear and the urge to survive. Sometimes they come about because of a psychological need for peer approval. Under extreme conditions, death wishes, provoked by a guilt reaction when one sees friends killed, have driven soldiers to extraordinary action. But heroism is not a term exclusively reserved to describe valorous acts performed on the battlefield. A mother who devotes her life to the care of a disabled child is, in many respects, every bit as much a hero as the soldier who sacrifices his life to save the rest of his unit.

The military has designed numerous training exercises that simulate combat in order to prepare its soldiers for the real thing. Exposed to the intense ordeals of fictitious battlefields, the participants rehearse over and over, yet they know that the enemy is not real and that death is not a real threat. No amount of exhaustive mental and physical training can guarantee desirable responses under live fire. It can only help to condition one to be able to withstand the onerous circumstances that might lie ahead.

For each of us, our initial encounter with the enemy in combat produced a godawful surge of adrenaline flushing through our systems, a wild thumping of the heart, a tightening of the gut, and a frantic urge to hit the ground in order to escape the round of fire that seemed to be destined to make a direct hit. We were young and death was only a somber and distant concept. We felt we were immortal, even in the rice paddies of Southeast Asia. Suddenly the reality of our transitoriness hit home.

Perhaps only a split second had passed during that moment of truth, but it felt like hours. The shock vanished. Everything we had ever learned up to that instant in time came rushing to mind. With a pronounced sensation of crispness and vitality, the mind pushed fear from its domain and focused on destroying the enemy.

In retrospect, it seems that in that brief instant of sudden realization the mind automatically journeyed to the subconscious level in which character resides. There, the mission and the safety of others involved in the mission were ratcheted high above personal needs. From this, we concluded that strength of character is clearly one of the common denominators among authentic heroes.

Likewise, in business it is character that separates the brave from the cowardly. It is what prevents people from yielding to less than honorable pressures and is the reason why a few Wall Street bankers and S & L and corporate executives jumped on the metaphorical grenades that meant the end of their jobs. These heroes risked their financial livelihoods and careers because they refused to accept unethical demands placed upon them by superiors, or to condone improprieties by associates, or to be party to a system imposed on them by inept governmental officials. Acknowledging the potential consequences of challenging the authorities, they exhibited a strength of character quite apart from those who remained silent or succumbed to the desire for personal gain of money, power, or simple job survival.

Conversely, on television, people formerly perceived of as heroes—respected politicians, judges, preachers, and leaders of Wall Street, banks, and S & Ls—broke down and cried when declared guilty of unethical behavior by courts of law. As the cameras rolled, the hero image dissolved, exposing an absence of character. Americans asked the question: How could they have possibly been considered heroes by so many?

Business battlefields are centered in the mind. On these battlefields, character is tested and retested under a kaleidoscopic set of situations and circumstances. Decisions are made to stand up courageously and be counted. And just as often, ethics are sadly compromised for personal advantage.

Although heroism cannot be taught, character can most definitely be developed. The very purpose of West Point is "to build leaders of character." The academy's "2002—and Beyond: A Road Map to Our Third Century," states that "character is more readily recognized than defined." It goes on to say that "a person with character has the judgment to know what is right and the courage to act on that knowledge. Character connotes not only moral and ethical excellence but also firmness, resolution, self-discipline, and judgment." The inner mettle that produces heroes, indiscernible though it may be to others, is rooted in individual integrity.

At West Point, it is believed that character is "the link between values and behaviors. . . ." Cadets are taught that "hard work, study, and challenging experiences are necessary to build strong and honorable character. . . . The better you understand yourself, the easier it is to exercise your will and self-discipline, and the more you strengthen your character." This follows the character-building steps listed in *Military Leadership*, which are applicable to individuals at all stages and in all stations of life.

- Assess the present strength of your values and character.
- Determine what values you want to promote.
- Seek out missions and situations that support developing such character.
- Select a role model who demonstrates the values and character you are trying to develop.

Business should adopt similar programs to encourage the development of character and, when appropriate, reward those who demonstrate the courage to take a position on what they believe to be right. These are society's true heroes: the special individuals who are prepared to risk all to defend ethical and moral principles.

# ·10·

## AWARDS AND
## DECORATIONS
### "A Minimal Expense
### for Resolute Service"

As young cadets we gazed with deep admiration at the colorful array of ribbons pinned to the uniforms of combat veterans. We stood in awe of their heroic deeds, which at the time seemed beyond our wildest dreams. Even the narrowly arched cloth shoulder patch with the word *Ranger* boldly embroidered in black against a yellow background seemed remote and to many of us, symbolized having become a man.

At that time, financial gain and attaining a position of social prestige offered no incentive whatsoever. As cadets, our bodies, minds, and souls were committed to a brotherhood guided by Duty, Honor, Country. West Point prepared us for this idealistic service, yet it was only on the battlefield that we could genuinely be baptized into this very select order of manhood. If need be, we were prepared to shed blood and risk death in order to win the medals of valor that would admit us to the round table of courageous warriors who had preceded us in wars throughout history. It may sound like an idea from the pages of *Camelot,* but such were our youthful dreams within the gray fortress walls on the Hudson.

At West Point we learned that the decorations we coveted had become an integral part of the military only during this century. Resentment toward monarchical Europe and its decadent custom of awarding military trinkets had long ago precluded such practice in America. Only the Badge of Military Merit, later called the Purple Heart, was authorized to be awarded for service in the American Revolution. During the Civil War, the sole authorized award was the Medal of Honor, which was later redesignated with new criteria for extraordinary valor at the risk of life in confronting an enemy. But, like the impure European system that decorated royalty for political reasons, the Medal of Honor too was bastardized. For instance, during the Civil War all 864 men of the 27th Maine Regiment were awarded the medal for extending their garrison duty in Washington, D.C., after the expiration of their one-year enlistment.

The policy of a single decoration remained until World War I. Believing that awards and decorations would have a positive impact on morale and increase motivation, the military gradually multiplied them until they grew, unfortunately, to the point that they exceeded the use for which they were created. Compounding this negative effect was an ever-increasing emphasis on awards to determine career advancement. Many decorations were awarded for fabricated acts of gallantry, and as we observed in Vietnam, it was not uncommon for higher ranking officers to order subordinates to recommend them for valorous decorations although the closest they had come to combat was to be strapped in a helicopter several thousand feet above the battlefield. Such fraudulent acts naturally diluted the meaning and importance of awards and left many of us skeptical about the awards system overall and the authenticity of certain individuals' purported actions.

Still, despite this skepticism, even today first impressions of individuals in uniform are undeniably often influenced by the presence or lack of ribbons. A modest, stamped piece of bronze and accompanying one-inch ribbon is a minimal expense for resolute service to country and the risk of life during war. Such an award costs next to nothing to manufacture, and still it proves to be one of the most effective methods to motivate and reward exemplary deeds.

Businesses, by contrast, tend to reward deserving employees with promotions, bonuses, and perks. However, other forms of recognition have also proven effective in encouraging and rewarding outstanding performance. A properly planned, communicated, and controlled awards program similar to that which is used in the military can be highly effective to achieve these goals. Some considerations in implementing such a program may include:

1. Awards should be used to create psychological incentives. What counts is not necessarily the monetary value of the award as much as its meaning to the recipient and its impact upon his or her peers.
2. People want to believe in what they are doing and need to be rewarded for their efforts.
3. Awards should foster a team environment in which individuals are able to show what they have done for their fellow teammates.
4. It is essential to limit the number of awards given. Too many awards compromise the program.
5. Awards should be given in a public forum for maximum effectiveness.
6. Award presentations should be timely. When appropriate, a program should have on-the-spot awards for specified activities or achievements.
7. Various levels of awards should be designated and explained to all personnel. Understanding their meaning and requirements will enhance the image of recipients in the minds of their peers and will provide motivation for others to achieve.
8. Some basic awards above and beyond bonuses and salary adjustments that might serve as a foundation for a program within an organization include:

   • Service awards for longevity (five-year increments) such as a pin, with monetary awards accompanying service beyond twenty years.
   • Retirement pins, pens, or watches accompanied by a framed certificate and monetary gift. The award should reflect the organization and be presented with the

employee's family present in a public forum and with appropriate publicity.

- Monetary or gift certificates. These should be reasonable so as not to create unrealistic expectations. The monetary award should be accompanied by a certificate suitable for framing.
- Certificates of Achievement. These should be endorsed by the board of directors or senior management. They should be signed and presented by a senior officer.
- A special distinctive award for exemplary and unusual excellence or actions. Only one or two should be awarded per year. This award should be in the form of a unique pin that reflects the style of the organization or its CEO and accompanied by a framed certificate and monetary award, presented publicly and with appropriate publicity. This award should be approved by the highest authority in the company.

Within the purview of awards, businesses have traditionally rewarded individuals with benefits or perks commensurate with their position in the corporate hierarchy. These may include reserved parking spaces, limousine services, company cars, executive dining room privileges, and memberships in country clubs. Although such perks are relatively effective as an incentive to increase one's level of responsibility, there is a danger that they may exacerbate an informal caste system where those may exist. Whether such a perceived situation is real or merely psychological, efforts should be taken to reduce obvious inequities among management and between management and staff.

Simple policies that abolish reserved parking, eliminate separate dining privileges except where customers must be entertained, discontinue luxury company automobiles, and offer memberships only in clubs that provide a direct benefit to the business contribute to a harmonious work environment. As the military axiom states: an officer eats the same food from the same tray as his troops—after they have first been served. This approach can go a long way in building loyalties and esprit de corps in the business world.

# ·11·

## ESPRIT DE CORPS—
## MORALE
### "Understanding Human Nature"

Morale, in most cases, can be traced back to the commander or executive who is responsible for inspiring enthusiasm, devotion, and esteem in individuals and in a group. At West Point, we were taught that this begins with understanding human nature and maintaining a sensitivity to the needs of others.

Many business managers, as we noted in chapter four, disregard the opinions, thoughts, and feelings of individual employees. The sense of family that is typified in the military is often lacking in business, and consequently many employees are emotionally numb to their jobs. The office or the factory is merely a place they spend eight to ten hours a day in order to survive. The only loyalty that exists is to the paycheck and doing whatever is required to avoid jeopardizing its continuation. This sad reality is experienced by all too many people. And yet, the work conditions that breed such discontent can easily be altered at no additional expense. By appealing to employee's needs, individually and collectively, discontent and a crippling sense of unimportance can be transformed into enthusiasm, pride, and loyalty and trust in their companies and managers. This, in turn, results in increased and dedicated job performance and quality of production. As Napoleon discovered, "morale is to the material as four is to one." In other words, morale is four times more important than weapons and equipment in determining the outcome of battles.

Morale and esprit de corps are part of the military tradition, in which there exists a mutual bond among individuals, a loyalty to associates and leaders, and the will to fight. Esprit de corps, or team spirit, as stated in FM 22-100, embodies "the soul, the state of mind of the unit . . . the overall consciousness of the unit that the unit personnel identify with and feel a part of." In the military, units are required to eat, sleep, and sometimes fight in desolate jungles and deserts for weeks and months on end, which means that commanders must continually keep at a high priority the monitoring and improvement of morale. To support this task, the Army developed a Positive Command Climate program. It outlines techniques that leaders can employ to build trust among the men and between the men and leaders and to engender an ambiance of fairness, teamwork, and open and candid communications.

The program, which was created after we both had departed the service, details specific actions a leader can take to build a positive command climate. These concepts, noted in *Manual of Common Tasks,* are not altogether new; they are very similar to the leadership fundamentals that were ingrained in us as cadets.

1. Communicate a sense of vision or focus.
2. Maintain a proper focus in all training activities.
3. Establish high, attainable, clearly understood standards.
4. Encourage competition against standards rather than each other.
5. Allow subordinates the freedom to exercise initiative.
6. Establish accountability at the proper level.
7. Show confidence in subordinates.
8. Encourage and reward prudent risk taking.
9. Achieve high performance through positive motivation and rewards.
10. Underwrite honest mistakes.
11. Share decision making with subordinates when appropriate.
12. Give clear missions and indicate where subordinates have discretion and where they do not.
13. Listen to your subordinates and seek their ideas.
14. Demonstrate concern about the welfare of subordinates.

15. Establish and model high standards.
16. Practice what you preach.

As obvious as these ideas may appear, many managers tend to ignore them. Even the basic need to listen to employees is often neglected, particularly when their opinions represent opposing viewpoints. Some managers take advantage of their superior positions and refuse to address uncomfortable issues that might prove them wrong or that might demand changes to the way certain tasks have always been done. Others live in an isolated world, unaware of dissension among the lower ranks.

The list of problems such as these could go on for pages. Many of them are caused by insecure egos, prejudiced attitudes, a perception of inferior intellect among subordinates, and complacency resulting from doing the same job for too long. The fact is that management often has no idea that subordinates are frustrated and unhappy, and that they—management, that is—are the primary cause of a depressed workplace.

Some executives do recognize they have an inability to delve into the workers' psyches and understand their thinking. They acknowledge that Management by Wandering Around (MBWA), i.e., by eating in the company cafeteria, by rolling up one's sleeves on the production line, may not truly uncover the underlying feelings that prevent job satisfaction. In such cases, employee attitude surveys, when administered anonymously, have proven to be a reliable gauge by which one can better understand employees' opinions and feelings. Although these specific considerations are not ones developed by the Army, we have found them helpful in evaluating organizations, regardless of any personal assessment of morale. Following is a list of the points that should be addressed in creating and conducting such a survey.

## Employee Attitude Survey

1. Purpose. To analyze the current morale of the company and to develop plans and actions to improve those areas determined deficient.

2. Management accepts all comments, even though they may be critical. No vindictive actions will be taken as a result of the survey's responses.

3. Management and selected members of employees' group should agree to the survey's objectives and design of questionnaire prior to implementation.

4. Design of the questionnaire is critical. A typical form might include general information on respondent; reaction to current policies and practices (general multiple choice); written option (may include comments about job, supervisor, company, and other areas of concern). Survey forms are available at human resource firms for selected areas including job demands, working conditions, pay, confidence of management, adequacy of communications, chances for growth, and effectiveness of administration.

5. To reduce biases due to potential inside influences or perceived intimidation, the survey should be administered by a qualified disinterested third party.

6. The survey should be administered during the work day to attain maximum participation and ensure anonymity.

7. Corrective action should be initiated as soon as possible based on an analysis of the survey, with feedback communicated both in writing and orally to participating employees. This is perhaps the most important aspect of the entire process. It validates the importance placed by management on the survey, acknowledges the participation and responses submitted by the employees, and offers specific solutions to problems affecting morale.

An objective evaluation of survey results should indicate the state of an organization's health from the perspective of employees and should pinpoint areas that need to be addressed. The CEO and his top executives should fully endorse the program and ensure that a follow-up plan is developed, communicated, and implemented on a timely basis.

# ·12·

# EXPERIENCE
## "Amorphous Yet Vital"

There is no such thing as a course on experience at West Point or any other school. Experience and what it brings can be difficult to define and to evaluate. Although it is a rather abstract concept, its implications in daily life are very real.

This is perhaps never more apparent than in war. As young infantry commanders, we were constantly confronted with situations that required an immediate decision. Some of course were more life threatening than others, yet all, in one way or another, called on experience to be factored into the decision equation. In some cases, particularly early on as we each went through our first tour in combat, we were fortunate to have even survived, considering the shallowness of our practical knowledge.

For both of us, it was not until our second tour in Vietnam that a confidence born of grappling with on-the-ground situations began to take hold. The rustle of water, the crack of a twig under foot, strange smells, nervous peasants' eyes—experiencing all these firsthand added a new dimension to the environment. Contrary to the law of diminishing returns, the longer we were exposed to combat, the better we were equipped to survive as our bases of experience grew.

Experience is a concept that defies scientific description and evaluation. It is most accurately described as a feeling one has, a sense of certainty about one's capability. Similarly, a lack of experience evokes a helpless sensation. Mental analysis of new situations is inevitably influenced by ideas and prejudices resulting from previous encounters with similar situations and circumstances. The broader the base of one's experiences, the more realistic and far-reaching are its influences, and thus a more confident feeling arises. The narrower the scope of experience, the less profound is one's range of perception, and the greater the sense of anxiety.

No one knows exactly how experience is stored in the brain, yet we have immediate access to the information it contains and constantly scour its files for past solutions applicable to present and future situations. When we draw on past experience to make decisions, our search for an appropriate course of action does not yield merely a single precise response, but is accompanied by a multitude of memories, or reference points. For example, the simple mention of the word *foxhole* triggers unique feelings and ideas that extend far beyond the image of a hole in the ground. For those who have experienced digging and being inside a foxhole, the mention of the word sends a wave of memories: the bloody calluses on one's hands from pounding a trench shovel into the rocky slopes of a hill ridge; torrential rain pouring into the muddy cavity, rising higher and higher until one's shivering body is immersed; the cramped, confining space that makes it impossible to sleep. Merely reading about such an ordeal in a book while seated in a soft, comfortable living-room chair at home cannot possibly evoke such imagery. No amount of study at West Point or any other service schools could bring us to understand war and how we would respond to it. It was not until we were in the trenches and the enemy started shooting at us that we knew. It is experiencing the total spectrum of sounds, smells, images, tastes, and anxieties that life's involvements consist of that form the amorphous thing we call experience.

In its effort to build capable leaders of its officers, the military has found it most effective to transfer individuals from one assignment to another every two to three years, in terms of both function and geography. Thus the officers accumulate an increasing wealth of diverse challenges. Unlike many businesses, the military rarely keeps a person in the same position for thirty years, repeating the same work year in and year out. Assignments usually vary from troop command to staff positions all around the globe, interspersed with increasingly advanced education. It is a process that has proven effective in developing experienced leaders capable of defending the nation.

Similarly, well-run corporations rotate managers into new positions in which they are required to master steep learning curves, and having done so, are moved into another unfamiliar managerial slot. This building-block approach helps to expand individual perception and to increase intimate understanding through hands-on participation while helping a manager to develop judgmental skills eventually sufficient to steer the company. Just as the word *foxhole* conjured a multitude of images, so should a list of business words and ideas trigger knowledge gained from past situations that resulted in both positive and negative outcomes. Managers confront increasingly more difficult challenges until they are prepared for the ultimate assignment of CEO, which might be most aptly characterized as Chief Experience Officer.

Certain fundamental experiences that bring about a sense of values, decisiveness, and the ability to handle and motivate people are transferable to most courses of life. Likewise, specific skills and building blocks are transferable from industry to industry. However, one must be willing to learn the language indigenous to a new environment to make the most of one's past experiences so that they will contribute effectively to the new tasks at hand.

# ·13·

## TRAINING
### "Repetition Creates Reliable Responses"

When we were young officers, military life seemed to be a never-ending series of repetitive training sessions. Our restless psyches squirmed under the peacetime regimen of rehearsals upon rehearsals with no live action. How many times did we need to jump out of an airplane or charge up a hill to master the routine? It was like being a fireman who never did anything more than incessantly polish a fire pole that he would never slide down to rush to battle a blaze—a waste of time and education. Driven by the energy of youth, like many of our contemporaries we yearned for a real war to break the monotony of simulated battlefields and mock enemies. It wasn't until we were immersed in armed conflict that we fully grasped the meaning of the saying that "the more you sweat in training, the less you bleed in war."

In combat, performance on the battlefield is directly linked to how well individuals are trained in their jobs and as a group. As in team sports, practice builds competence, coordination, trust, and confidence. It is the cornerstone of combat preparedness, a discipline that "permeates everything a military organization does," as noted in FM 22-100. History has shown that those who were not thoroughly prepared for fighting are the most likely to fall, whereas those who are properly trained tend to survive and win.

Operating on the premise that repetition creates reliable responses, training works on a building-block principle that subjects participants, singly and collectively, to increasingly more complex situations. However, too dogmatic an approach, as has sometimes been employed in certain areas of military training, can suppress independent thought and result in robotic, by-the-book behavior.

In business, every day can be seen as a continuing battle, and training is often considered unproductive and as an unneeded expense. At the most, training is conducted only for entry-level personnel. Managers are reluctant to part with the key employees needed to attend training, even for a few days, since they are considered essential to operations. What management too often fails to recognize is that stagnation in skills, particularly in those industries where technology is constantly changing, can hinder a company's ability to compete. A properly planned and executed training program can assist in correcting this problem.

Military members are experts in training. They follow a centralized planning concept with decentralized training execution. Individuals are instructed by leaders and members of their units and develop the skills required to complete the tasks of their jobs. The programs and standards are underwritten by commanders from the top down, and they personally participate in the planning, execution, and assessment of these programs. It is common for ranking generals to observe training operations and imprint their own individual style in an operation's content and procedures. This personal involvement creates a climate conducive to effective training and eliminates conflicting priorities. As noted by Peter Drucker, the Japanese follow a similar course and emphasize the importance of training: "The Japanese method of making workers take responsibility for their jobs and tools is continuous training. All employees keep on training until they retire. Weekly training sessions are regular and scheduled parts of their work. The sessions are usually conducted by the employees and supervisors themselves rather than a trainer."

In accordance with its structured training program, the military requires that instructors adhere to standardized written lesson plans to ensure uniformity and proper planning for individual presentations. These lesson plans serve as a guide for the class and

66

are usually prepared by the trainer and approved by superiors. When appropriate, "dry-run" rehearsals are conducted under the supervision of superiors prior to their live performance. In cases of informal instruction, detailed lesson plans may not be required, but the basic procedures remain the same, and the trainer must be thoroughly proficient and prepared. The guide outlined below lists the areas to be covered in a lesson plan and details the kind of information that should be included within each area. Using this basic military format, business can develop their own plans to meet their individual needs.

## Lesson Plan (insert an appropriate title)

*Purpose:* This should clearly state why the training is to be conducted.

*Audience:* This area should explain who will be receiving the training.

*Objective:* List the activities that each participant is expected to be able to perform at the end of the training session. Be specific, as this will be used to evaluate the effectiveness of the training. There is no point in training unless it will benefit the individual and the organization, so remember to keep the objectives realistic and achievable.

*Prerequisite Training:* This area should state what the students must already be able to do prior to receiving this instruction.

*Training Guidance:* In this area, explain how the training can be accomplished.

  1) Preparation.

    a) *Trainer.* Explain what he or she should read or review, how to set up the training area, give reminders as to the development of a training outline, communicate with participants as to pre-class requirements, responsibilities, and material needed.

    b) *Students.* List what they should read, review, prepare.

    c) *Resources.* List all that are available for the instruction.

  2) Presentation. Explain your objectives and present material.

3) Main points to be stressed. Outline all points to be emphasized in descending order of importance.
4) Performance evaluation. Will this training be evaluated? If so, explain how.
5) Training tips. Include here any additional material or techniques that will add to the presentation.
6) References. List the references to be used in preparation for the training. These should be noted for validation of information presented and future use by the participants.

Training in business can be conducted within an organization as well as in outside environments. Although high-level managers typically attend formal seminars and symposiums outside the organization covering a broad range of subjects from leadership skills to technical knowledge, there are significant opportunities within an organization for continuing education at all levels. The financial situation of the organization often dictates the frequency of such participation, and many managers view such development programs as an extraneous expense. However, many progressive companies have instituted in-house training programs conducted by company personnel, which, similar to those used by the military, have proven to be an effective and ultimately economical method to train and cross-train employees.

Because of the rapid replacement of personnel inevitable in combat, the military cross-trains its people so that the effectiveness of a unit will not collapse with an exploding mortar round. Similarly, businesses should not be brought to an abrupt halt because certain people possessing key skills are absent. Cross-training should be an ongoing responsibility of management to ensure backup expertise for all critical positions, including that of CEO. As is practiced in the military, executives should constantly train their lieutenants to be able to replace them.

# ·14·

# MANAGEMENT OF CHANGE
## "The Right Balance Between Regenerative Creativity and the Stability Required for Longevity"

A brief tour of West Point, fifty miles north of New York City, might lead one to question how the academy has anything to offer businesses on the subject of management of change. Nestled in the sleepy hollows of the Hudson River, West Point's grounds are dotted with bronze statues of great military leaders who seem to stand watch over an institution encapsulated in a time warp of tradition for nearly two centuries. It may seem rather difficult to imagine any form of change transpiring within this immutable bastion.

Both of us recall that at West Point we were inundated with a plethora of regulations and procedures on how to follow, to lead, and to react under a multitude of circumstances. And yet, in spite of its almost unending list of methodologies, West Point neglected to address one of the most critical components of leadership: the ability to manage change. Although in our cadet days we were subjected to an array of challenging circumstances, we were taught to minimize and overcome them simply through repetitive, trained responses.

At the time when we entered the academy, this was the pervasive attitude throughout the military. Status quo was all-important and was obstinately guarded by suffocating layers of stagnated

middle-management majors and colonels. At the slightest suggestion that might make waves that could affect their security and
retirement, which is to say at the suggestion of any innovative
ideas, predictably they stepped on the defenseless offenders,
squelching any ambition to instigate change. This unprogressive
mentality was largely the reason why many intelligent junior officers evacuated the military after serving their years of obligatory
duty. During this period, the American military lazily basked in
the glory of its World War II victory, content in its belief that it
could win any conventional war by employing the same weapons
and tactics used to defeat Germany and Japan. Clearly, change was
not a priority.

Crisis, however, is nearly always the impetus for change, and
Vietnam was just that for the military. Several years after the withdrawal of American troops from Southeast Asia and after years
of intensive introspection, a new era of leadership emerged within
the military. Advanced degrees from civilian universities became the
normal prerequisite for promotion to senior officer rank, and the
glut of inept middle managers were retired or purged. The new
rising leaders recognized that to respond to changing times and
future needs, the military had to change within.

Concurrently, West Point too underwent a soul-searching
process, examining its role in the development of the nation's
young leaders and how to adapt to change. After five years of
preparation, a plan was presented in 1990. The foreword written
by Lieutenant General Dave Palmer, superintendent of the
academy at that time, in "2002—and Beyond: A Road Map to Our
Third Century," capsulized the study's findings: "Time moves.
Traditions grow and fade. Institutions either evolve or face obsolescence. To remain unchanging in a changing world risks decay
from irrelevance. . . . To change capriciously, chasing whim or fad,
risks decay from irresolution. The challenge—a timeless one for
West Point—is to find the right balance between regenerative creativity and the stability required for longevity."

The process addressed the academy's shortcomings and the criti-
cisms it had received, and through it, West Point concluded that
Army leaders of the twenty-first century "will require the mental

agility to grasp a unique battlefield situation under conditions of uncertainty and chaos, the creative ability to devise a practical solution, and the strength of purpose to execute their plans. Despite rapid technological change, however, human nature will change hardly at all. . . . In a world infused with great and accelerating change—change so dramatic as to be potentially paralyzing—Army leaders must, as the summation of all attributes, be able at the very least to cope with such change; at the very best, to shape and direct it."

All of America witnessed the results of the military's new mentality in Desert Storm. Demands for fixed political goals and policies prior to the risk of a single soldier's life; the deployment of sufficient men, equipment, and materiel to ensure a decisive victory with minimal casualties; and an audacious execution of tactical plans were all signs of change, even under a cumbersome bureaucracy. While most observers were amazed at the high precision and enormous destructive capabilities of modern weapons, equally impressive were the men operating the high-tech war machines. These were the manifestations of how management of change can affect a situation at all levels. And they were living examples of how business can learn from the military.

Unfortunately, America's major auto manufacturers were less responsive to the changing times. Had Japan not recognized what consumers want and delivered them a product at an aggressively competitive price, Detroit's auto industry most likely would still be arrogantly mired in their refusal to change.

Change is not a new phenomenon. It has always been a factor in business, but recently it has taken on a new dimension. As John Naisbitt and Patricia Aburdene pointed out in their book *Megatrends 2000,* "in the decade of the 1990's we are moving from managing control to leadership in accelerated change. . . . Simply doing things faster will not work. The leadership of constant change requires people who are comfortable with ambiguity, although most would prefer order."

Ideally, change should mean a positive challenge and experience for an organization and its people. However, it should not be used as a quick fix for short-term financial gain, nor should it be imposed merely for the sake of change itself, nor should a com-

71

pany wait until a crisis before taking positive action. Management of change means making concerted efforts to recognize and identify factors that forewarn a need for alteration to product selection and design, manufacturing, marketing, and distribution. Furthermore, it means continually updating plans and setting aside capital reserves to achieve the flexibility needed to be able to shift when times demand change. Perhaps most important, it calls for discarding the vested ways of doing business when they have lost their potency.

Yoshimichi Yamashita, president of Arthur D. Little in Japan, has warned his nation's business leaders that the old Japanese way, although successful in global competition, is quickly approaching obsolescence. He formulated a prescription for change, which we should take keen notice of as we analyze our competitors and devise our future plans for battle in commerce.

- Stop believing every dilettante who proclaims that Japanese management is Number One. Japan's doing well only because its national industrial structure is efficient and its society monolithic. These two advantages could easily become less significant if Japanese management doesn't shift character.
- Adopt a more rational approach to strategy and administration. Stop wasting energy with too many people doing too few things too many times (e.g., Japanese distribution system).
- Guide the organization away from values that "only the Japanese can understand." Emphasize that the new model of corporate culture (notably, that of U.S. multinationals such as Coca-Cola and IBM) blends domestic and imported approaches.
- Stop "Japanizing" ideas from the West and start Westernizing Japanese management.
- Give up feudalism and go modern by discouraging the Japanese concept of "group ego," which covers everything from the monopolistic *keiretsu* to the in-crowd, company ego.
- Recognize individual talent in the company and rally around the creative spirits. Stop hammering your mavericks.

72

- Speak English and stop ostracizing those managers who speak English "too well."

In our rapidly changing new world order, the threat of obsolescence has taken on new meaning for all competitors. Today's marketplaces no longer enjoy the safety of protectionist walls, nor do today's consumers purchase only those products made in their native homeland. Who survives in the future will show who effectively managed changes—and who did not.

# ·15·

# RULES OF THOUGHT
## "Inspire Positive Action"

When we read Bob Woodward's *The Commanders,* we were particularly impressed by a list of rules and maxims General Colin Powell uses in making decisions. More than a mere framework, they are real guides to developing leadership traits.

General Powell kindly agreed to having his list included in this book. His prompt and sensitive reply to our request attests not only to his generosity but to his commitment to leadership as well. His ideas are indubitably of value for any and everyone to develop or refine his or her own rules.

### Colin Powell's Rules

1. It ain't as bad as you think. It will look better in the morning.
2. Get mad, then get over it.
3. Avoid having your ego so close to your position that when your position falls, your ego goes with it.
4. It can be done!
5. Be careful what you choose. You may get it.
6. Don't let adverse facts stand in the way of a good decision.
7. You can't make someone else's choices. You shouldn't let someone else make yours.

8. Check small things.
9. Share credit.
10. Remain calm. Be kind.
11. Have a vision. Be demanding.
12. Don't take counsel of your fears or naysayers.
13. Perpetual optimism is a force multiplier. [In the military, one always seeks ways to increase or multiply forces.]

Woodward included two more Powell aphorisms in his book: "Sometimes being responsible means pissing people off," and "You never know what you can get away with unless you try."

Lists such as these are usually gradually formulated over years of experience. At first they may be comprised solely of inspirational quotes from writings such as Kipling's *If.* But as one's personal philosophy takes form, other people's rules tend to be replaced, one by one, with one's own. For the West Point graduate, certain principles of integrity and respect for others that are ingrained at the academy cast an indelible influence on evolving codes of behavior.

Unlike a New Year's resolution in which one almost always ends up including a promise that gets broken, these rules represent standards by which one lives one's life. In one fashion or another, most successful leaders write down their rules and position them where they will serve as a constant reminder. Colin Powell conspicuously placed his on the center of his desk under its glass cover. Others tape them to their bathroom mirrors so that they are seen every morning. Some carry them printed on small cards in their wallets or in their agenda books. As cadets, we had personal checklists inserted in the transparent inner lining of our hats.

Regardless of a list's specific contents, it should inspire positive action and discourage negative thought. It is not a wish list. Some may feel that to call it a set of rules or maxims is constricting and may prefer to call it an "interself memo" or a "conscience reminder." Whatever name it goes by, this is a proven technique useful to anyone who is interested in self-improvement.

# PLANS
# AND
# PROCEDURES

# ·16·

## DECISION MAKING
### "Made by Individuals, Not by Committees"

Decisiveness in today's dynamic and global corporate world is being crippled by a management-by-committee mentality. Fewer and fewer true leaders who are willing and capable of making the tough decisions are to be seen in the hallways. Rather it is the almighty quarterly earning report, influenced by short-term financial pressures, that manipulates corporate decisions.

To alleviate much of the anxiety and uncertainty that deters one from making critical decisions and to encourage executives to come out from behind the protection of consensus votes, the business community would be well advised to adopt some of the decision-making fundamentals practiced by the military.

Great military leaders throughout history have exemplified a common trait: the vision and confidence to make decisive, timely, and courageous decisions. Although their personal styles may vary greatly, accomplished leaders share an uncanny ability to cut through nonessentials quickly and to take action on matters critical to a mission. As Wess Roberts noted in his book *Leadership Secrets of Attila the Hun,* even in the days of Attila the Hun, it was recognized that "rarely are there perfect decisions . . . the best decisions are the more prudent of the logical alternatives."

Few people have an inherent talent for decision making, but like leadership, it is a quality that can be developed. The military designed a systematic tool to assist all commanders in the decision-making process. Simple in format and logically constructed, the military's plan can be used effectively by even the lowest rung in the chain of command. This problem-solving process, outlined in FM 101-5, consists of:

1. recognizing and defining the problem;
2. gathering the facts and making assumptions needed to determine the scope of solutions to the problem;
3. developing possible solutions to the problem;
4. analyzing and comparing possible solutions;
5. selecting the best solution to the problem.

Valid assumptions are essential to this decision-making equation. Just as is true in business, the outcome of military battles can depend on the degree of accuracy in such assumptions; just one invalid supposition, as history has demonstrated, can result in unnecessary casualties and defeat.

The formation of assumptions and the gathering of facts are tasks normally performed by staff officers, roles often viewed as distasteful yet necessary for those who aspire to command. Like staff positions in corporations, they are depicted on an organizational chart with a box connected to the commander by a dotted line, indicating no formal line authority. Their sole responsibility is to serve the commander. Senior staff officers can seem a continual nuisance to subordinate commanders, since they often assume the power of the commander and create seemingly unnecessary work simply for the sake of appearing important. Regardless of the disdain that may be felt for them in their advisory positions, they serve very critical roles in the decision-making process.

In wartime, staff officers are confronted with a continual barrage of information, unknowns, partial or erroneous data, and a fluid and uncertain battlefield. They must nevertheless remain constantly aware of the pivotal impact of timing on possible courses of action.

Forecasting optimum timing is more an art than an exact science as many planners and economists might want the less informed to believe. Often gut feelings, tempered by experience and common sense, are more accurate than the sophisticated computer programs that dominate in the business and military worlds.

One needn't have been a military strategist to understand the influences of weather and troop buildup on the timing of Desert Storm prior to August 1990. It was obvious that a major offensive could not be launched until heavy armor had been positioned in staging areas near the battlefront. Furthermore, it was clear that, from a weather standpoint, a "window of opportunity" existed between January and April, when the sandstorms and heat would subside. Thus January was selected for initiation of the air strikes, while the ground war would not commence until the enemy had been sufficiently weakened by the air forces and prior to the beginning of inclement weather.

To achieve advantages over the enemy, the military employed a basic decision-making method that called for a realistic assessment of all key issues and recommended actions. They also recognized that overanalysis of the ifs and whens of timing decisions could be paralyzing and equally as detrimental as action taken at the wrong time or not taken at all. The basic steps involved in the method, detailed in Annex B, are just as applicable to business decisions.

1. *Problem.* Make a concise statement of the problem.
2. *Assumptions.* List any assumptions that will be necessary for a logical discussion of the problem.
3. *Facts bearing on the problem.* Examine the undeniable facts having influence on the problem or its solution.
4. *Discussion.* Give a detailed analysis of all relevant factors, including the advantages and disadvantages of possible solutions to the problem.
5. *Conclusions.* Draw conclusions from an analysis of the relevant factors, possible solutions to the problem, and factors affecting these solutions.
6. *Action recommended.* Make one or more statements about how to implement the conclusions; the action recommended must be consonant with the conclusions.

It is essential that commanders encourage their staffs to analyze thoroughly all pertinent information, to develop conclusions, and most important, to articulate recommended alternative solutions, not just the problem. The commander must always be aware that the final decision and accountability belong, ultimately, to him.

Many business organizations diverge from the military's method of decision making and attempt to solve problems by committees or consensus. Generally, this process obviates the making of a decision by the manager and serves as a means for individuals to deflect any risks, as it allows them to hide behind the veil of the committee. This consensus approach is espoused by more liberal management, with the stated intent of building teamwork and a sense of individual worth. Unfortunately, what happens in the process is that there is a breakdown in accountability for decisions. It is this lack of accountability that perhaps more than anything else can present a serious obstacle to effective decision making.

Decision making in business environments is often less structured than in the military. Businesses frequently have developed problem-solving methods that reflect the structure and discipline of the individual organization and—especially—the leadership styles and personalities of the CEOs. However, regardless of the particular approach used, well-respected business leaders concur that problem solving should be done according to a standardized method and that important and critical decisions should be made by individuals, not committees. To borrow from an old military axiom, "Counsels of war [committees] don't fight."

# ·17·

## STAFF STUDY—
## DECISION PAPER
### "Present Solutions,
### Not Just the Problem"

RTP—Read the Problem—was drummed into our heads for four years at West Point. We both vividly recall having examination papers returned with a bold, red *RTP* printed in big letters on it, indicating we had responded with a perfectly valid answer but had interpreted the question erroneously. When during combat we once received pallets of the wrong type of ammunition for our unit's weapons, we immediately knew that some rear echelon staff officer (or "REMF," as we called them—the acronym for a phrase unfit for print) had failed to understand our request. Fortunately, we were able to rectify the situation and we received the proper ammunition before the enemy discovered our disadvantage. This life-threatening situation was dramatic testimony to the importance of the military's principle that problems must be identified and understood before any action is taken.

The military's Staff Study, the backbone of most nontactical staff actions, is designed to minimize ambiguities. It explicitly states that problems must be clearly defined prior to addressing them. This assures the commander of the parameters of the problem and ensures that the study's analysis and conclusions will not deviate from the stated problem. Like most of the military's methodologies, the Staff Study follows a clearly defined format, yet it allows sufficient flexibility to enable the preparer to form his own thoughts and conclusions.

The Staff Study is usually initiated by the commander and assigned to an action officer responsible for the problem area in question. It calls for an identification of the problem, discussions of alternate solutions, and recommendations based on pertinent facts and assumptions. The study can be brief, no more than two or three pages, accompanied by backup data in its annexes. The Staff Study is customarily submitted in written form by the action officer to his superior, but it may also be submitted orally or, when time constraints are pressing, it may be reduced to a one-page summary.

Typically the study begins with a concise statement of the problem. The action officer commences the process by brain-storming on a broad spectrum of possible solutions. Although the ideal solution would be based solely on facts, since decisions will affect future events, assumptions (discussed in detail in chapter twenty-two) are formulated to fill gaps where facts are not available. This entails researching a variety of sources of information.

Depending on the scope and significance of the Staff Study, the action officer may need to consult with other staff officers for their concurrence or nonconcurrence to the study's findings. Because the tasks assigned to the different staff members within a command are diverse—they may include, for example, operations, logistics, intel-ligence, and administration—nonconcurrence to conclusions and recommendations will often occur. In most cases, nonconcurrence derives not from divergent interpretations of facts, but from differ-ences in priorities and opinions about assumptions and about the importance of certain assumptions to the overall scheme. Each staff member naturally tends to view his or her function as being of great magnitude. Any such disagreements should be resolved prior to the formulation of conclusions and recommendations, and when they cannot be worked out, statements of nonconcurrence should be attached to the study's annex.

The Staff Study format, as depicted in FM 101-5, should be viewed as a map for a mental process. It teaches subordinates to think from the outset about how to develop sound assumptions, alternatives, conclusions, and recommendations. It expedites the decision-making process, whether the recommendations are accepted in full, in part, or not at all. See Annex C for a Decision-Making Sequence.

## Staff Study Format

1. *Problem.* A concise statement of the problem in the form of a mission stated in the infinitive area (e.g., to determine . . .). If the problem is complex, show the scope.

2. *Assumptions.* List any assumptions necessary for a logical discussion of the problem. Assumptions are used in the absence of factual data to constitute a basis for the study and to broaden or limit the problem. The assumption, while not a fact, must have a basis in fact. Assumptions are always written in future or conditional tenses.

3. *Facts bearing on the problem.* Statements of undeniable fact having influence on the problem or its solution. Care is exercised to exclude unnecessary facts because they confuse the issue. Some facts may be uncovered during the research, while others are inherent in the directive assigning the problem. Facts should be listed in a sequence which permits logical development in the "Discussion" paragraph. A reference should be provided for facts which are not a matter of common knowledge.

4. *Discussion.* Detailed analysis of all relevant factors, including the advantages and disadvantages of possible solutions to the problem. In this paragraph, the author sets down in a clear and concise manner an objective analysis of the data secured during research. In a lengthy or a complicated staff study, this paragraph may be only a summary, with the details included in a discussion annex. Care must be exercised in setting down the discussion to ensure that each item is placed in proper perspective.

5. *Conclusions.* Present the conclusions drawn from the

analysis of all relevant factors, all possible solutions to the problem, and all factors that affect these solutions. Conclusions must follow logically from the previous paragraphs. No new material should be introduced in the conclusions. At least one solution must directly answer the problem statement.

6. *Recommendations.* One or more statements addressing what should be done to implement the conclusions. Recommendations must be in agreement with the conclusions. The staff action must be complete. If it is recommended, for example, that a letter be signed by the commander, the actual letter should be attached to the study as the first annex.

In business, subordinates often present only problems and not recommended solutions, and superiors who condone this behavior effectively play a large role in decreasing their initiative to solve problems. As a result, not only is the superior inundated with a continual barrage of problems, but equally detrimental, the subordinates are deprived of opportunities to develop decision-making skills essential for managerial advancement.

The military's Staff Study steps are useful in leading to the formulation of business decision papers. Below is a sample outline of a decision paper concerning the reduction of administrative personnel costs. Although this outline is not all encompassing, given that all situations are unique and demand attention to different areas, it nonetheless illustrates the effectiveness it has in guiding one for the preparation of studies that lead to objective and prudent decisions.

## Decision Paper

*Subject: Cost reduction.*
1. *Problem.* To eliminate nonessential positions for the purpose of reducing administrative personnel costs.
2. *Assumptions.*
   a. There will be no reduction in efficiency and effectiveness by the removal of certain positions.

b. Reduction will increase profitability.

3. *Facts bearing on the problem.*
   a. Administrative costs are in excess of functions performed.
   b. Certain positions cover duplicate tasks.
   c. Administrative jobs do not contribute to sales.
   d. Medical and other employee beneficiary costs are increased.
   e. A larger and more efficient computer is needed.
   f. Additional office space is needed.

4. *Discussion.*
   a. Analysis of advantages and disadvantages of terminating selected positions.
   b. Financial projections after reduction in costs.
   c. Cost/benefit analysis.
   d. Timing considerations.

5. *Conclusions.* Draw conclusions based solely on discussions in paragraph four.

6. *Recommendations.* State recommendation(s) and support the decision. Recommendations should include timing and other critical factors and supporting reasons.

Although the Staff Study format is used primarily for military situations of a nontactical nature, its format can be applied to most circumstances and conditions, nontactical or tactical, military or business. The Commander's Estimate of the Situation, which appears in the next chapter, is another type of decision paper that specifically addresses the military and business battlefields.

# ·18·

## ESTIMATE OF THE SITUATION
### "Who, What, Where, When, How, and Why"

In Vietnam a unit adjacent to ours had a reputation for charging enemy dug-in positions without first prepping the area with artillery and air support. They bragged that no Vietcong was too tough for them. To us, this John Wayne–fixed bayonet approach was destined to result in an unwarranted loss of human lives. Before long we heard that half of the unit was killed, including the unit commander, when they attacked a heavily fortified enemy regiment. Had the commander been realistic in assessing the enemy's strength and capabilities, as well as his own vulnerabilities, the suicidal nature of such tactics would have been obvious.

This bravado—or stupidity in our view—clearly illustrates how crucial it is to minimize individual biases in the evaluation of possible courses of action. The Commander's Estimate of the Situation is a systematic procedure carefully designed to do just that. It provides the commander with a checklist to collect and analyze information in order to arrive at intelligent decisions on how to accomplish a mission. The Estimate, as described in FM 101-5, gives an objective picture of the battlefield and summarizes "the significant aspects of the situation, including both facts and assumptions, and indicates how the means available can best be used to resolve the problem or to accomplish the mission." It results in decision statements of who, what, where, when, how, and why. Because it is thorough and logically sequenced, it demands that the commander focus on all pertinent facts and assumptions involving a particular problem in order to arrive at sound conclusions.

Making decisions means combining logic and reasoning based on scientific methodologies with gut feelings. No matter how a decision is finally reached, subjectivity is bound to influence, to one degree or another, the process and outcome. This is true not only for the military, but even more so for business.

For example, we were commissioned by a manufacturer to help extricate them from a situation of untenable loss in a foreign country amounting to millions of dollars. As we conducted our investigation, we discovered that the company had applied a formula it had found to be successful in the United States without fully considering the new market's culture and ways of doing business. Just as was true of the Vietnam incident, a thorough, unprejudiced estimate of the situation would have warned the company's management of the folly of transferring the American product style abroad and would have provided solutions to ensure success.

Although the Commander's Estimate was formulated to serve military operations, its logic is valuable for analysis of virtually any situation and is especially beneficial to business. It can be as comprehensive as time permits and the situation demands and, like the Staff Study, can be written or presented orally, depending on the circumstances and the urgency. Often it addresses only the key points, since many aspects have already been discussed or covered by SOPs (Standing Operating Procedures). A more detailed format is provided in Annex D.

## Commander's Estimate of the Situation

1. *Mission.*
2. *The Situation and Courses of Action.* In this paragraph, the commander considers all elements and aspects of the situa-

tion that influence operations and formulates feasible courses of action.

3. *Analysis of Courses of Action.* Analyze each of the courses of action formulated in paragraph 2 to determine their advantages and disadvantages, to incorporate improvements, to determine requirements for supporting fire, and to define requirements for any other actions in conjunction with the course of action. This is accomplished by war gaming the course(s) of action.

4. *Comparison of Courses of Action.* Compare courses of action analyzed in paragraph 3 and reach a conclusion on the best course of action.

5. *Decision (Recommendation).* Use the course of action that offers the best probability of success as a basis for the decision. The decision provides for the accomplishment of all elements of the stated mission. The elements of who, what, when, where, how, and why are present in the course of action.

Typically, the Commander's Estimate is war gamed when time permits in a sandbox, a three-dimensional, to-scale depiction of the terrain, prior to execution, which is discussed in chapter thirty-one. This allows the commander to have a bird's eye view, in three dimensional form, of the known and assumed elements affecting the solution to the problem.

Based on the military model, the following outline for a marketing decision paper can serve as a checklist to prevent managers from straying from critical decision paths into emotional mine fields and to lead them to sound business conclusions. Again, this outline is intended to be adjusted to satisfy the needs of different industries and their own methods of operation.

## Marketing Decision Paper

1. Statement of objectives for this paper.
2. Situation.

a. Characteristics of targeted marketplace.
   1) Description of geographical location(s).
   2) Economic, political, social, psychological, and seasonal considerations of area.
   3) Demographic analysis.
   4) Customer profiles and buying habits.
b. Competition (separate description for each competitor of significance).
   1) Names and profiles.
   2) Product profile to include state of the art.
   3) Market positioning and share.
   4) Strengths, weaknesses, and vulnerabilities.
   5) Location of manufacturing and primary base of operations.
   6) Location and description of distribution center(s).
   7) Marketing and promotional techniques. Advertising methods to include media usage.
   8) Distribution network and methods of sales.
   9) Customer image and perception.
   10) Sales and merchandising support techniques.
   11) Financial resources and conditions. Note if subsidiary of larger corporation, or other forms of relationships.
   12) Estimated current R & D commitment and history.
c. Own situation. State analysis of own current situation as relates to the points noted above.
d. Relative competitive powers. Based on an analysis of the above data, assess the general overall comparative strengths and weaknesses.
e. Competition capabilities. Statement of the competition's capabilities to determine what the competition can perform to influence the accomplishment of the objectives.
f. Own capabilities. State own capabilities and the options of own courses they provide.
3. Analysis of courses of action. List and analyze each of the courses of action based upon own situation and capabilities. Determine the advantages and disadvantages of these courses of action to methods available to improve their capabilities.

War gaming these options can help disclose strengths, weaknesses, and vulnerabilities of courses of action under consideration. It can identify areas in need of modification.

4. Comparison of courses of action. Compare courses of action analyzed in paragraph 3.
5. Decision (recommendation). Select the course of action that offers the best probability to accomplish the objective successfully. When and where appropriate, modify to enhance its capabilities.

Business tends to be less objective than the military in its analysis and decision-making processes, partly because of differences in goals and disparities in mind-set. What's more, egos, particularly those that are heavily influenced by the promise of power and money, can be major forces that result in emotionally based and reckless decisions.

Given the danger such subjectivity can have on decision making, it is crucial that a procedure be developed to guide the collection and analysis of pertinent intelligence from which conclusions can be drawn free of the influence of individual needs or prejudices. The Commander's Estimate, time-tested under the most stressed and shifting circumstances of war, when tailored to suit a business interest's particular needs, provides a clear plan to steer the course to sound conclusions.

# ·19·

# ANALYSIS OF THE BATTLEFIELD— MARKETPLACE
## "Ask 'What If This Happens?'"

The battlefield is perceived by most as an expanse of terrain upon which two forces clash. Waterloo, Gettysburg, Dunkirk, and now Kuwait come to mind. But the real battlefield consists of a small space no larger than a melon. This six-inch area is located in the cranium between two ears. That is where synapses fire and the battles that will be fought on earthly terrain are planned, where fears are contained, and where the euphoria of victory and the agony of defeat are experienced.

At the outset of Desert Storm, Saddam Hussein's psyche was discussed at length by the coalition planners prior to the finalization of an offensive strategy. Specifically, they addressed how Hussein was likely to respond to a broad assortment of initiatives. A psychological profile of Hussein showed him to be a malignant narcissist with a total disregard for life other than his own. It further showed him to be thoroughly paranoid of the subordinates surrounding him, which resulted in a fragile vertical command structure that depended on all orders originating from one source. Thus it was deduced that if communications between Baghdad and the front lines were cut, the defending forces would not act without authorized directives. In short, cutting the lines of communication would paralyze the massive Iraqi fighting forces.

In business, to meet the objectives of marketing battles, one must understand the minds of the consumers. With the barrage of advertising directed at the public, it can take an excessive amount of promotional dollars to capture their attention. In this ongoing struggle for market shares, or merely to outsell the competition, management, regardless of the size of its organization, should first attempt to enter into its consumers' minds. Concurrently, management should try to think like the competition—the enemy—in order to gain valuable information that will enable them to position their forces intelligently, or to withdraw if the risk appears too great.

In this era of intense global competition, American and foreign marketplaces have been inundated with international companies. No longer are battles waged primarily on home turf. A quick glance at the products found in a typical living room illustrates the wide range of nations competing for the consumer's dollar. Clearly, the need for intelligence gathering and methods for reaching reliable conclusions has never been greater.

In order to ensure the comprehensive collection and evaluation of pertinent information affecting the military battlefield, West Point teaches a method used in planning stages by the Army. The Intelligence Estimate of the Situation, as it is called in FM 101-5, analyzes all relevant factors pertaining to battlefield conditions and enemy forces, including their psychology and will to fight.

Although the modern battlefield has evolved to a state of high technology in which planning specialists work with matrixes and computer models, the guide is every bit as useful today as it was fifty years ago. The Intelligence Estimate, similar in format to the Commander's Estimate, considers various scenarios from the most to the least likely and repeatedly asks the question "What if this happens?" Comprehensive and logical, it is a checklist for the collection, formulation, and analysis of vital intelligence that enables commanders to choose the most favorable course of action. See Annex E for a more complete format.

# Intelligence Estimate

1. *Mission.*
2. *The area of operations (the battlefield).*
   a. Weather.
   b. Terrain.
   c. Other characteristics.
3. *Enemy situation.* Discuss enemy information which will permit later development of enemy capabilities and vulnerabilities and the refinement of these capabilities into a specific course of action and its relative probability of adoption.
4. *Enemy capabilities.* Based on all the previous information and analysis, develop and list enemy capabilities (e.g., attack, defend, employ nuclear and chemical weapons). The listing provides a basis for determining those capabilities that the enemy can adopt as specific courses of action and their relative probability of adoption.
5. *Conclusions.* Based on all the previous information and analysis, conclusions are stated concerning the total effects of the area of operations on friendly courses of action; the courses of action available to the enemy, to include their relative probability of adoption; and the side effects of the enemy vulnerabilities that can be exploited. These conditions assist in the selection of a friendly course of action.

By translating military nomenclature into appropriate business terms, the Intelligence Estimate will provide a helpful format for market analysis, to be used by management in their planning stages. Although meeting consumer demand is the primary objective of business, management should gain as thorough as possible an understanding of the competition and their current and anticipated courses of action. Naturally, the following basic list will vary according to the needs of individual industries.

# Market Analysis

1. *Objective.* A brief statement of what the analysis intends to achieve.
2. *Marketplace.*
   a. Physical characteristics. Describe the physical marketplace, including location, demographics, consumer buying habits, market peculiarities, fashion trends, seasonal considerations (if any), transportation and ecological factors, etc. Discuss other factors influencing the marketplace such as politics, economics, import restrictions, and taxes.
   b. Consumer. Discuss the nature and peculiarities of targeted consumer, including buying habits, psychology, age, sex, sociological/economic profile.
3. *Competition.* Describe existing competition, including quality and state-of-the-art of products, market share, distribution, sales force, consumer loyalties, reputation, location of manufacturing plant and distribution centers, media support, financial conditions, history of doing business in targeted area, products in development, anticipated future products, estimated dates for introduction of new products, weaknesses, vulnerabilities, condition and modernization of factories, labor unions, tactical habits. Discuss strengths and weaknesses of management.
4. *Competition Capabilities.* List those capabilities competition can adopt as specific courses of action and their relative probability of adoption, including introduction of new products, market expansion, promotional blitz, relocation of factories and distribution centers, strategies to defend market shares. Enumerate what, when, where, and strength for each capability. List evidence to support anticipated capabilities. Note reasons when a capability is not likely to be used, or when it is not possible.
5. *Conclusions.* Discuss the effects of marketplace on own courses of action; courses of action available to competition

and their relative probability of adoption; the effects of competition vulnerabilities that can be exploited.

The foregoing analysis is but one tool available to management for its decision-making process. Like the marketplace, it is dynamic and continually updated as new information about the marketplace is gathered.

# ·20·

# ANALYSIS OF THE CONSUMER
## "The Ultimate Objective"

To the military, the consumer is a paradox. Consumers are perceived by business as a friendly force, yet attacked as if they were the enemy. Strategies and tactics are constantly being devised to win their support. Marketing and promotional campaigns read like battle plans to invade hostile enemy territories. The methods employed by the military in these operations are devised to analyze the enemy's human dimensions and in similar operations are developed by business to understand targeted customers.

The military defines human dimension as the "overall mental, moral, and physical willingness and capability of soldiers (leaders and troops) to do their duty on the battlefield. . . ." By contrast, the human dimension of the consumer, from a marketeer's viewpoint, relates to particular needs and buying habits, individual and collective. These needs vary from culture to culture and change depending on social/economic circumstances. In analyzing and attempting to satisfy these needs, or lack thereof, businesses will either succeed or fail in their efforts to sell.

Winning the hearts and minds of the indigenous populace in regions on which a battle will take place has always been a critical consideration in the military's planning process. It is of particular importance when invading foreign countries in which the populace is diverse in mind-set and background. The Intelligence Estimate outlined in chapter nineteen demonstrates the applicability of the military's format to analyze and make conclusions about a physical marketplace and competition. It can also be used as a guide to collect data, develop assumptions, and draw conclusions about consumers, both domestic and foreign, and about methods to gain their support.

Too often companies ignore the fact that product styles and selling techniques effective in one culture may not be appropriate for another. They attempt to impose their methods for success on new markets and are surprised when they don't work. Such miscalculation is by no means limited to United States firms. A large cosmetics company based in Asia, for example, asked us to assess their United States marketing strategy. For several years they had been unsuccessful in their efforts to penetrate the American marketplace. It didn't take long to understand why. They had failed to take into account the different tastes of the foreign market; only Asian models appeared in their promotional material. Although the models were of course attractive, American consumers simply did not relate to them.

Failure to fully comprehend the consumer prior to launching a product has resulted in countless warlike situations in which companies have incurred heavy losses. In most cases, many of the obstacles could have been anticipated by thorough analyses. The following modified estimate can help management to do just that and to understand and address the peculiarities and needs of consumers.

## Consumer Analysis

1. *Objective.* A brief statement of what the analysis intends to achieve.
2. *Marketplace.* Describe the physical marketplace, including location, demographics, economic and social/religious conditions affecting purchasing, fashion trends, seasonal considerations, competition, and other parameters and peculiarities of the targeted market.
3. *Consumer.* Profile existing consumer to include age, sex, psychology, social/economic status, disposable and discre-

tionary income, fashion conscience, buying habits, etc. Describe who purchases and for whom; where they purchase; importance of convenience; impulsive buying and willingness to wait; effects of pricing, terms and delivery schedules; advertising and marketing influences, etc. Analyze in detail existing and potential consumer resistance. State whether reasons for resistance are religious, ideological, or social.

4. *Courses of Action.* Describe alternative courses of action to satisfy consumer needs. Analyze each from the viewpoint of the consumer. Analyze the company's capability to produce and deliver products that meet these needs.

5. *Conclusions.* Based on the analyses of the company's capabilities, the marketplace and consumer needs, develop a course of action that will economically satisfy consumer demands.

Remember: the real business battlefield is in the mind of the consumer. Success in designing and positioning products for a specific market requires an intimate, thorough understanding of the mind-set of the consumer.

# ·21·

# LOGISTICS
## "Position Supplies Near the Battlefield Prior to Operations"

In World War II, the German First Panzer Army penetrated deep into the southern sector of the Soviet Union to capture the critical oil fields in the Caucasus, only to be stopped in their tracks due to a gasoline shortage. When General George Patton's Third Army tanks, in pursuit of a retreating German division, suddenly ground to a halt, they too were out of fuel, so the enemy escaped annihilation. Germans on the eastern front and Patton on the western front simply outran their supply lines.

Theoretically, had the logisticians been given sufficient time and resources to position vital supplies forward to support the charging tanks, the Caucasus's oil resources would have been taken by the Germans and Patton may have rumbled, uninterrupted, all the way to Berlin.

Forty-five years later, the logistics displayed in Desert Storm were considerably better planned and executed. Never have so many people and so much equipment and materiel been marshalled, transported, and positioned in support and staging areas from such a great distance in such a short period of time. After the shooting began, supply depots were leapfrogged forward by helicopter, assuring the timely availability of fuel for the gas-guzzling heavy tanks and helicopters. It was a Herculean feat deserving of study by business and military people alike.

Recognizing the importance of Saddam Hussein's logistical umbilical cords, the Allies concurrently worked around the clock to destroy them and their support centers from the air for the duration of the Gulf War. Unable to resupply and communicate with these isolated units, many of the Iraqi forces, completely demoralized, surrendered en masse. Clearly, logistics—or the lack thereof—plays a pivotal role in the outcome of war.

Vital to military logistics is the procurement and timely movement of equipment, supplies, and people. Within this structure, lines of communications are but one facet of a vast system extending all the way back to individual factories in the United States. However, as history has taught us, regardless of the sophistication of the logistics and weaponry, unless sufficient fuel, ammunition, and essential materiel reaches combat forces when needed, the system is ineffective.

To reduce this risk, supplies should be positioned near the battlefield prior to the commencement of operations. A thorough analysis of logistical factors affecting the accomplishment of a mission including materiel and personnel must be made. Site locations for staging supplies and maintenance operations should be planned. Lead times for initial stock fulfillments and resupply should be calculated, and order and shipping dates should be established to ensure the availability of sufficient supplies and that the pipeline is full to safeguard against the worst case scenarios. In offensive actions on a mobile battlefield, arrangements should be made for support elements to move forward concurrently with advancing tactical forces in order to keep lines of communication as short as is prudent.

The Logistic Estimate of the Situation, which is similar to Commander's and Intelligence Estimates, is designed to assist in the development of plans that determine the positioning and movement of supplies and equipment. It is a method used to analyze the logistic factors that affect the feasibility of tactical courses of action under consideration. Concise and logical, like the other estimates, it provides the commander with a comprehensive guide to analyze and develop courses of action. An outline more extensive than the following is extracted from FM 101-5 and provided in Annex F.

# Logistic Estimate of the Situation

1. *Mission.* The restated mission by the logistic commander.
2. *The situation and considerations.*
   a. Intelligence situation to include characteristics of the area emphasizing aspects which may effect the logistics effort, enemy strength and disposition, enemy capabilities affecting the mission, and logistic activities.
   b. Tactical situation to include present disposition of major tactical elements, possible courses of action, and projected operations.
   c. Personnel situation to include present disposition of personnel and administrative units and installations that have an effect on the logistic situation; projected developments within the personnel field likely to influence logistic operations.
   d. Logistic situation to include present status of maintenance capability, repair time factors, resupply availability, service and transportation capabilities and problems, labor and restrictions, facilities and construction, and other.
3. *Analysis.* Analyze all logistics factors indicating problems and deficiencies. The result of analysis for each course of action should provide both logistical and tactical impact.
   a. Sufficiency of area. Determine if the area under control will be adequate for the combat service support operations. Will it be cleared of enemy units; will other units be sharing the same area; will boundaries remain unchanged, etc.?
   b. Materials and services. Includes maintenance, supply, services, transportation, labor, facilities, other.
4. *Comparison.*
   a. Evaluate logistic deficiencies and list the advantages and disadvantages with respect to the accomplishment of the mission.
   b. Discuss the advantages and disadvantages of each course of action under consideration. Include methods of overcoming deficiencies or modifications required in each course of action.

5. *Conclusions.*
   a. Indicate whether the mission can be supported.
   b. Indicate which course(s) of action can best be logistically supported.
   c. List the major logistic deficiencies that must be brought to the commander's attention. Include specific recommendations concerning the methods of eliminating or reducing the effect of these deficiencies.

In business wars, distribution serves a function similar to the military's sustainment of operations. The positioning of adequate inventories and supplies near the areas of battle is essential to an uninterrupted process of sales and service support. Depending on the nature of the business, this may entail positioning a distribution center or warehouse close enough to the customers to resupply them on a periodic or as-needed basis. Unlike the military, businesses are driven by profit motives; consequently, distribution costs are carefully scrutinized, since they are often viewed as not contributing directly to sales. Still, businesses must be careful to be responsive to customer needs: you can't sell from an empty shelf.

Computerized inventory systems have advanced to become practically an exact science that can aid management in minimizing capital tied up in inventory and assure that adequate stock is on hand. These programs rely on input of accurate data and reasonable assumptions regarding future demand. Yet despite such sophisticated technology, businesses often fail to position stock in sites that allow for delivery at acceptable costs when and where the products are needed.

Using the Logistic Estimate as a format, we developed a plan for a foreign client considering the United States national market for the first time. The company manufactured a line of consumer products in its native country and was struggling with many unanswered distribution questions. Since the company was not experienced with American culture and its unique methods of doing business, we included the full spectrum of considerations that a United States company would analyze to determine the feasibility and weigh the costs and benefits of expanding into a foreign marketplace.

## Distribution Analysis

1. *State the purpose.*
2. *The situation and considerations.*
   a. List United States ports of entry, distances and time from port of origin, and respective distances to targeted marketplaces. Indicate responsiveness and costs of port facilities and customs and FDA inspectors.
   b. List potential distribution sites in United States. Indicate distances to marketplaces, availability of transportation and respective costs.
   c. Discuss availability of warehouse space and costs, labor costs, and state and local taxes.
   d. Discuss methods of sales to include manufacturer's representative organizations and company sales force.
3. *Analysis.* Analyze all factors and considerations indicating benefits, problems, and deficiencies. This should include ports of entry, distribution centers, and methods of distribution and sales.
4. *Comparison.* Compare advantages and disadvantages, benefits and weaknesses, of considerations evaluated in analysis.
5. *Conclusion.*
   a. Indicate whether the purpose can be economically supported.
   b. List major logistical problems to be brought to decision maker's attention. Include recommendations on methods to eliminate or reduce these deficiencies.
   c. Indicate which port of entry, warehouse location or multiple locations, methods of distribution and sales can best facilitate the logistic requirements. Relate this to time, costs, and other economic and convenience factors.

After conducting the analysis, we recommended a port of entry, a centralized location for a distribution center that provided transportation systems for prompt delivery to its customers, labor resources, a distribution and sales network, methods to satisfy customs and governmental regulations, and other major factors. Included with each area of concern were anticipated expenses. Air freight from point of origin was disqualified as a primary method of shipment because of its high cost. We also calculated the lead time necessary to position all of the above elements in place and to ensure sufficient inventory on hand prior to the commencement of marketing and sales activities. This involved positioning near the marketplace an amount of inventory that would fulfill the most optimistic sales scenarios while allowing for resupply shipping time with built-in safety factors.

This business expansion was in many ways similar to a military invasion of enemy-held territory. Using the logistical outlines above, we were able to evaluate all pertinent factors that might affect the efficient and timely flow of merchandise from the factory to customers. As is true of most first-time entries into any marketplace, the supplier had one shot—and it had to be accurate. Failure to maintain a proper level of inventory in appropriate locations can defeat critical opportunities for success and leave even the most talented businessperson's operation stranded—like General Patton's tanks stuck in the mud waiting for fuel.

# ·22·

# OPERATIONS PLAN—
# BUSINESS PLAN
## "A Road Map from Here to There"

In the fall of 1990, as Bob Woodward reported in his book *The Commanders,*

> Key portions of the ground campaign [Operation Desert Storm] had been developed by half a dozen junior officers in their second year at the Army Command and General Staff College at Fort Leavenworth. These majors and lieutenant colonels, nicknamed the "Jedi Knights," had been sent to Saudi Arabia to apply the elements of advanced maneuver warfare—prodding, flanking, surprise, initiative, audacity—to the war plan. Working in a small top-secret corner of Schwarzkopf's headquarters, they had applied the principles of the Army's unclassified 200-page operations manual. Chapters 6 and 7 on offensive operations were built around concepts established in General Grant's 1863 Civil War campaign at Vicksburg. Instead of attacking directly into enemy fortifications, Grant sent his troops in a wide maneuver around the Confederate front line, and then attacked from the side and rear. This indirect approach was deemed the best way to beat Saddam.

The results speak for themselves.

Of the various skills one develops in the military, planning is one of the most transferable to business, once one acquires a fluency in the language of business. Military personnel and West Point graduates are disciplined to think constantly in terms of strategic and tactical positioning and maneuvers.

As the preceding chapters have pointed out, in the preparation of a plan, the military considers all pertinent intelligence affecting the mission and repeatedly asks "What if this happens?" in order to anticipate all possible enemy and situational scenarios. The plan serves as a map to define present positions, future objectives, and the courses and methods needed to reach the objectives. A plan, in short, is a method or a scheme for action.

The military's list of criteria for developing a plan is fundamentally relevant to business at all levels in today's high-tech world. "A good plan," as FM 101-5 states,

1) provides for accomplishing the mission, which is the objective of all planning.
2) is based on facts and valid assumptions. All pertinent data have been considered for their accuracy, and assumptions have been reduced to a minimum.
3) provides for the use of existing resources. These include resources organic to the organization and those available from higher headquarters.
4) provides for the necessary organization. It clearly establishes relationships and fixes responsibilities.
5) provides for personnel, material, and other arrangements for the full period of the contemplated operation.
5) provides for decentralization. It delegates authority to the maximum extent consistent with the necessary control.
6) provides for direct contact permitting coordination during execution between all levels.
7) is simple. It reduces all essential elements to their simplest form and eliminates those elements not essential to successful action. A good plan also eliminates all possibilities for misunderstanding.
8) is flexible. It leaves room for adjustment because of operating conditions and, where necessary, stipulates alternate courses of action.

9) is coordinated. All elements fit together, control measures are complete and understandable, and mutual support requirements are identified and provided for.

Taking these standards as a basic guide, the military has formulated a logical progression to be taken in the development of plans. The procedure, known as the Planning Sequence, helps the commander and staff to assure the timeliness of plan completion and the comprehensive collection and analysis of facts and assumptions to support decisions. The sequence consists of steps that to a large extent are merely common sense. Too often management fails to follow any logical course at all to prepare business plans. The following Planning Sequence, as listed in *Staff Organization and Operations,* can help management to tailor a suitable approach to their planning process.

## Planning Sequence

1. Forecast to determine probable requirements. Forecasting is the analysis and evaluation of facts and trends to determine probable requirements. Its purpose is to predict what may occur.
2. Study probable requirements and establish priority of future preparation. This involves an analysis of forecast requirements and assumptions to determine the probability of their occurring, so that priorities can be established for further planning and preparation.
3. Study the implications and interrelationships of the probable requirements to formulate an assumed mission, or missions.
4. Analyze mission to determine the specific tasks to be performed, their complexity, and their relative importance.
5. Establish guidelines for specific tasks. Planning guidance keeps all planners moving in the same direction at the same time.
6. Prepare planning studies. Planning studies determine the key factors in an undertaking and explore these factors in detail.
7. Select course(s) of action. An outline plan is prepared for

each retained course of action. Because preparation for all reasonable contingencies is the aim of planning sequence, considerations of courses of action involves more than elimination of all but one course of action. Several feasible courses of action may be retained so that the command is prepared for all likely contingencies.

8. **Prepare complete plan.** The outline plan provides a framework from which all details necessary to build a complete plan may be added. These details may come from the original estimates and studies of the problem or from new studies developed as the planning progresses.

9. **Conduct rehearsals.** Conducting rehearsals when time, resources, and security permit is a good practice and allows for timely cancellation, revision, or refinement of plans.

Two basic methods were taught at West Point when we were cadets to plot the time and distance between current positions and future objectives. The Backward Planning Method starts from the objective and works backward. It entails having a specific completion or "drop dead" date. Interim completion dates are designated for intermediate points along the critical path to complete the mission by a targeted date.

The second method is used when there are no time constraints on completing the goal and when each event is predicated on completion of the previous task. It begins with today's position and moves forward in a logical sequence to various intermediate points to the final objective.

Both techniques help identify tasks and conditions required to accomplish the mission. Essentially planners must attempt to interpret the future. Thus the formulation of assumptions based on a variety of considerations, as noted in chapter twenty-two, are vital to the accuracy and thoroughness of the final plan.

The written plan should be simple and concise and address only those aspects essential to the mission. Discussions of matters unrelated to the mission serve only to increase the probability of misinterpretation and to cause confusion. The battlefield is like a chessboard on which pieces seldom remain in fixed positions. The plan, accordingly, must be continually updated as the variables change.

The Operations Plan (OPLAN), the military's counterpart to the business plan, is, as stated in FM 101-5, "a plan for operations extending over a considerable space and time and usually based on stated assumptions. It may cover a single operation or a series of connected operations to be carried out simultaneously or in succession." Most important, it focuses on considerations that will lead to the successful accomplishment of the mission. As FM 101-5 indicates, "it may be put into effect at a prescribed time, or on signal, and then becomes the operation order." Annex G gives a complete outline for an Operations Plan.

## Operations Plan

1. *Situation.*
   Information of the overall situation essential to subordinate commander understanding of the current situation.
   a. Enemy Forces. Composition, disposition, location, movement, strength estimates, identification, and casualties.
   b. Friendly Forces. Information concerning friendly forces.
   c. Attachments and Detachments.
   d. Assumptions. Include those situations/conditions that the commander believes will exist at the time the operation plan becomes an operations order.
2. *Mission.*
3. *Execution.*
   a. Concept of Operation. A statement of the commander's visualization of the execution of an operation from start to completion—how the selected course of action is to be accomplished.
   b. Specific tasks to be accomplished by each element of the command charged with the execution of tactical missions.
4. *Service Support.*
   A statement of the combat service support instructions and arrangements supporting the operation that are of primary interest to the units and formations being supported.

5. *Command and Signal.*
Instructions to command and to the operations of communication-electronics.

The business plan is comparable to the OPLAN in its raison d'être. Whereas business is profit oriented and the military is mission directed, it is fitting that the business plan focus on matters that can be reduced to financial data. The information included in the business plan should provide management with sufficient means to make sound decisions.

One of our first tasks upon entering the business world was to create a plan to raise capital for a start-up company. Although we scoured public libraries and the business sections of bookstores for a reference containing a competent format to follow, we found no guide that would satisfy our requirements. We consequently devised our own, based on the Army's five-paragraph Operations Plan. Years later, having prepared hundreds of plans for businesses of all types and sizes, we still use the same basic format.

These plans provide the tool not only to raise capital and secure financial loans but, most important, to provide management with a blueprint for achieving goals. Lengthy discussions, which tend to stray into nonessential areas, often dilute the impact of a report. Thus the business plans we have formulated are intentionally concise and focused. The effectiveness of a plan cannot be measured by the pound. Management may further find it prudent to prepare two separate plans, each with a different level of detail: one for internal use in the operational decisions of the company and the second for potential investors and bank loan officers.

Consistent with this rule of conciseness, plans prepared for the raising of capital should not inundate potential investors with superfluous information. The more information, the more reasons they may find to turn down the proposal. Often there is a fine line between the right amount of pertinent information and too much. Unlike what many may suggest, preparation of a finitely detailed business plan, in this case, should not be the objective; raising capital is. If a concept jotted on the back of a napkin can convince investors to invest, then anything more is unnecessary and, in fact, may kill the deal. Regardless of the method and extent of communication, the business plan must demonstrate viability with reasonable, i.e., justifiable assumptions.

Following is the outline for the plan we formulated several years ago to help the start-up company mentioned above to raise capital. This plan remains as appropriate as ever today. It can be used for the preparation of most business plans, although the contents will of course vary to suit individual industries. The main difference between the business plan and the OPLAN is in paragraph seven, which portrays the venture's profitability through financial projections—an issue not relevant to the military. An even more detailed outline is provided in Annex H at the back of this book.

## Business Plan

1. *Executive Summary.*
   A brief statement describing:
   - Purpose of plan.
   - Date and state of incorporation.
   - Names of founders and present list of shareholders.
   - History of the development of the business idea into the existing company.
   - Summary of the company's financial history for the past five years to the extent data is available.
   - Existing and proposed business.
   - Summary of existing market and market potential, competition, state of the existing art, market needs and demands, cost and pricing, methods of selling and distribution, production methods and techniques, packaging, advertising and promotion.
   - Patents and other product protective measures.
   - Plan for product development.
   - Key points of the plan demonstrating the logic of making an investment in the company.
   - Present capitalization and pro forma after giving effect to proposed financing.

- Amount of money requested and proposed terms of the financing.

**2.** *Management.*
- Organization chart.
- Brief résumé of each key manager.
- Brief description of the function of each key manager and their respective annual salaries and profit sharing arrangements.

**3.** *Product Description.*
Product description to include size, weight, shape, quality, cost of production, price, state of the art, service support, convenience, durability, proprietary and patent rights.

**4.** *Product Development.*
Describe in detail R & D program to upgrade or expand product line, plans to broaden product base, financial impact of development program on sales, earnings, and cash flow.

**5.** *Manufacturing.*
Describe the manufacturing operation, existing and proposed capacity, and current levels of production.

**6.** *Marketing Strategy.*
Discuss in detail short- and long-term objectives, customer profile, distribution, sales force, packaging, warehousing, servicing, transportation, merchandising, promotion and advertising, terms and conditions of sales, other relevant information.

**7.** *Financial History.*
Capsulize balance sheets, profit and loss statements, and statements of sources and applications of funds for the past five years.

**8.** *Pro Forma Financial Statements.*
- Detailed description of premises and assumptions.
- Projected balance sheet for five years.
- Projected statements of income for five years.
- Projected statement of cash flow for five years with the first year on a monthly or quarterly basis.
- Break-even analysis.

Acute, perceptive planning in the modern business world means using a highly developed skill that originated in military campaigns. Like military strategists, business planners should always seek a viable way to achieve victory at the least cost of people and resources. There is a real art to successful planning, as noted in *The Business Idea*, by Gil Dorland and John Van Der Wal, published in 1978: "A strategist is a creative thinker whose work may be likened to that of a painter of fine art, except that his subject is a complex business structure; his paint, people and capital; the canvas, business opportunity; and the brush, his method of combining these elements into a profitable whole."

# ·23·

## ASSUMPTIONS
### "Spell the Difference Between Victory and Defeat"

In late 1953, the French Army had underestimated the resolve and tenacity of the Vietminh at Dienbienphu. They were surprised by the sudden downpour of artillery rounds from hills surrounding their valley positions. Peasant soldiers had managed to carry artillery guns on their backs, piece by piece, through the dense jungles and onto the high ground overlooking the battlefield. There they assembled the ordnance and won a decisive victory. The French had failed in making correct assumptions about the enemy's sagacity and resolve to fight. They ignored the fundamental of reaching into the mind of the enemy and attempting to think like them. Ten years later, in developing its own assumptions on North Vietnam, America ought to have learned from those prior miscalculations.

Businesses, similarly, often neglect to think like the competition. They become so engrossed in their own situation that they are blind to what the competition is doing until it is too late.

Many of the questions we ask new clients focus on the competition. Who are they? What is their slice of the market? What is the "state of the art" of their products? What are their methods of distribution and sales? How capable is their management? And on and on. These commonsense questions help draw a profile of the competitor's capacity and capabilities, basic knowledge from which assumptions are formulated. Questions about the intentions and long-range plans of the competition are of course difficult to answer, but by employing various intelligence-gathering techniques, it is possible to make some informed hypotheses.

Businesses can learn from the military in going through the process of anticipating the moves of the competition. Because the military battlefield does not have an element corresponding to the business consumer, this discussion is limited to assumptions about the enemy and competition. Still, assumptions about the consumer and other factors are by no means insignificant; in fact they are of prime importance in planning business wars.

Military assumptions, as we were taught at West Point, are "suppositions on current or future situations, assumed to be true in the absence of positive proof. In the absence of facts, assumptions are used to fill gaps in what is known about a situation." The accuracy of these assumptions in planning for combat are critical and may well mean the difference between victory and defeat, between the life and death of young fighting men and women.

A valid assumption, as defined by the Army's *Staff Organization and Operations* manual, "substitutes for a fact that bears directly on the problem. It must be capable of being justified or defended. Valid assumptions describe conditions that must be fulfilled before the conclusions can be accepted without reservations. If an assumption turns out to be invalid, the solution will be invalid." A necessary assumption, the manual continues, is one that is "essential for the solution of the problem. Each assumption must be tested against the question: Is this assumption absolutely necessary to the solution of this problem? If the answer is 'No,' the assumption is eliminated. Too many assumptions result in the problem being assumed away. There are times, however, when it is desirable to establish boundaries so as to limit the problem under consideration."

Although it is often criticized for lacking creativity in developing assumptions, the military goes to great lengths to uncover as much intelligence about the enemy as time will permit. This information-gathering process includes the questioning of indigenous people on and near the area of operation, monitoring radio signals and communications, high overhead radar surveillance, investigation of sources of materials and supplies, and review of previous engagements by the enemy with other forces, to name but a few activities.

Information of this nature, although it is often spotty and not always possible to confirm, is analyzed for validity and pertinence to the overall scheme of the battlefield. The results of the analysis of intelligence become key factors in the development of assumptions about the enemy's capabilities and probable courses of action. They are subsequently incorporated along with validated facts into the decision-making model, the Intelligence Estimate of the Situation, as outlined in chapter nineteen.

Assumptions are essential, and in fact possibly the most critical consideration, in the preparation of business decision-making models as well. Sales assumptions, the key to financial pro formas, are based on a variety of conditions affecting consumer demand, including competitive pricing, quality of production, availability, service support, and state of the art. Assumptions based on invalid intelligence can alter the entire outcome of an undertaking. Just as is true in the military, any business would be foolish to wander onto a battlefield without a plan that evaluates strengths and weaknesses of the competition.

For example, competitive products in development are carefully guarded secrets and, in most cases, unknown to the marketplace until officially launched. Assumptions, therefore, must be made from the enemy's point of view to determine what, when, where, and in what strength new products will be introduced. Depending on the conclusions, an assumption may be instrumental in making a decision to immediately dump existing inventory or to withdraw from the marketplace.

Businesses employ a number of techniques to gain pertinent intelligence. Quantitative market research studies reveal statistics about the consumer, the marketplace, and the marketability of the products in question. These studies usually are limited to controlled geographical areas that will provide management with indications of how other areas with similar demographics will respond. Properly prepared and executed, these studies are valuable sources for creating assumptions about the consumer and marketplace. However, they often fail to consider thoroughly the competitor's capabilities, probable courses of action, and long-range goals. Qualitative studies extract consumers' opinions about products to be introduced into the marketplace, but they fail to include information about the competition's willingness to fight.

The following guideline, founded on the military's procedures for developing assumptions about the enemy, provides a logical sequence for addressing the issue of competition.

1. Collect and examine as many relevant facts as possible. Use imagination in developing sources of intelligence. Validate facts with bona fide proof.
2. Collect and examine as many valid indications of competitors' intentions. Eliminate those that have no direct bearing on the problem.
3. Hypothesize assumptions to fill gaps between facts. Think like the competition to understand their point of view. In the case of foreign competition, seek knowledgeable counsel from advisers who comprehend the culture and have had experience in those markets.
4. As assumptions unfold into facts, modify other assumptions in accordance with new intelligence. The business plan should be continually updated to reflect changes in the competitor's capabilities and courses of action.

Just as is the military's practice, management should work to validate assumptions, using the enemy's point of view when appropriate, and retain only those assumptions that are vital to the solution of the problem. Indeed, "too many assumptions result in the problem being assumed away."

# · 24 ·

# ORDERS—DIRECTIVES
## "Issuing Orders Is Worth About Ten Percent — Ninety Percent Is in Execution"

During the Civil War, legend has it that General Robert E. Lee, in an effort to minimize confusion among subordinate commanders, required the soldier guarding his tent to read his written orders before they were issued. If the soldier didn't completely understand the instructions, Lee would rework them until the soldier fully grasped them.

Clarity, thoroughness, and comprehension are essential in combat orders. Courses on military arts taught at West Point are filled with historic accounts of entire armies annihilated because of misunderstandings of the commanders' orders. It is not hard to imagine the consequences when directives are not unconditionally clear.

The military defines an order as a "communication, written, oral, or by signal, which conveys instructions from a superior to a subordinate." Businesses tend to find the word *order* abrasive, and prefer to use the term *directive* or *instruction*. Military orders are generally more direct than business directives; for example, "Do it!" is commonly used by the military rather than the gentler civilian imperative "Let's get it done." Both, of course, have the same end result.

A military order implies that discretionary judgment is to be exercised by subordinates prior to its implementation. Nuremberg and My Lai clearly demonstrated that responsibility for immoral and unethical acts cannot be excused on the grounds that they were mandated by a higher command. West Point strongly advocates the right to refuse the acceptance of orders that violate accepted standards of morality and ethics: the "blind obedience" alibi has no merit.

To minimize the potential for confusion or misinterpretation of orders, the military has formulated specific guidelines for their preparation. Regardless of how they are communicated, orders should be presented as clearly as possible so that everyone within the organization, from the highest to the lowest level, will readily understand what is required of them. The Army's *Staff Organization and Operations* manual articulates many of the characteristics of a good combat order—which are the same characteristics of a sound business directive.

1. *Clarity.* The order must be thoroughly understandable.
2. *Completeness.* The order contains all the information and instructions necessary to coordinate and execute the operation. It must convey the purpose or intent of the commander so that subordinate commanders will be able to accomplish their mission without further instructions. An order also must include sufficient detail so that all subordinate commanders know what other units are doing.
3. *Brevity.* Unnecessary detail is avoided. However, clarity and completeness are not sacrificed in the interest of brevity.
4. *Recognition of subordinate commander's prerogatives.* The order should not infringe on the initiative of subordinate commanders by prescribing details of execution. Only under unusual circumstances, such as an operation requiring extremely close cooperation and timing, should a subordinate commander be told precisely how to perform an assigned task.
5. *Use of the affirmative form.* In the interest of simplicity and clarity, the affirmative form of expression is used throughout all combat orders. Sentences using the word *not* should be avoided.

6. *Avoidance of qualified directives.* Such expressions as "attack vigorously" weaken the force of subsequent directives in which a qualifying adverb does not appear. Such expressions as "try to hold" and "as far as possible" lessen responsibility.
7. *Authoritative expression.* The order reflects the commander's intention and will. Indecisive, vague, and ambiguous language indicates indecision and leads to uncertainty and lack of confidence by subordinates. The commander tells his subordinates in direct and unmistakable terms exactly what he wants to do.
8. *Timeliness.* Timely distribution of orders allows subordinate commanders sufficient time for planning and preparation. Concurrent planning saves time.

The format used by the Army in issuing orders is similar to the Operations Plan outlined in chapter twenty-two. Logical and comprehensive, the five-paragraph format is used as a foundation for the preparation and issuance of orders.

## Operations Orders

1. *Situation.* Information about the overall situation that is essential to the subordinate commander's understanding of the current situation.
2. *Mission.* A clear, concise statement of the task to be accomplished by the command and its purpose.
3. *Execution.* Concept of the operation with listing of specific tasks to be accomplished by each element of the command.
4. *Service support.* A statement of the combat service support instructions and arrangements supporting the operation that are of primary interest to the units and formations being supported.
5. *Command and signal.* Instructions relative to command and to the operation of communication-electronics.

Business directives take a variety of forms, from interoffice memos to bulletin board notices. Sometimes they are communicated in less conventional ways—for example, at a major Hollywood film studio, we witnessed executives first learning they had been fired when they pulled into their parking spaces and discovered their name had been eradicated from their reserved space. Termination notices have also been delivered, in effect, by repairmen ordered to change telephone extensions, much to the astonishment of the thus-far uninformed employee. In such cases, peculiar as they might have seemed, there was certainly no room for misinterpretation of the directive. However, business directives are most often riddled with ambiguities that lead to poor coordination and disastrous performance.

The Standing Operating Procedures, commonly known as SOPs, are an effective technique used by the military to reduce the potential for confusion. SOP, as defined in the Glossary, is a "set of instructions covering the features of operations that lend themselves to a definite or standardized procedure without the loss of effectiveness." In practice, SOPs reduce the contents of an order to its essentials, freeing commanders and their subordinates to focus their energy and time on the primary objectives, rather than diluting their effectiveness because of having to focus on efforts that should be routinely processed. SOPs will be discussed in greater detail in the next chapter.

President Kennedy's frustration over the apparent lack of attention that government bureaucrats paid to his directives, as related by General Clifton in the Introduction, is similar to the frustration many business leaders experience in their operations. In business, directives are routinely ignored well beyond their deadlines because of differences in priorities between managers. Even when they are acted upon, there is frequently a pronounced deficiency in follow-up activity.

General George Patton had a reputation for being a relentless taskmaster to his subordinates on following through with orders. He maintained that "issuing an order is worth about ten percent. The remaining ninety percent consists in assuring proper and vigorous execution of the order." And he firmly believed that "you can expect only what you inspect."

To ensure subordinates will be prepared to act on orders when they are issued, West Point teaches a military technique that gives preliminary notice that instructions will follow. These Warning Orders are usually brief and can be either oral or written.

This practice is easily applied to business situations: subordinates are warned that a directive addressing a particular subject is being prepared and will be delivered on or about a specific time and date. This alerts subordinates to be on the watch for its arrival and to conduct preliminary research and analyses. It also gives them time to clear their agendas in order to attend to the issue promptly when the order arrives. This forewarning minimizes aggravating inconveniences caused by surprises and unknowns. The result is a smoother operation, improved morale, and a greater attention to directives. Warning Orders can benefit just about any organization—and its employees, who will appreciate advance notice of what management is expecting of them. Annex I contains a detailed outline for a Warning Order.

# ·25·

## STANDING OPERATING PROCEDURE (SOP)
### "Reduces Confusion in Recurring Procedures"

We first encountered the term *SOP* on or near that momentous first day as cadets at West Point. Commencing all movement with the left foot was, we discovered, an example of an SOP of the simplest kind. Building on that fundamental procedure, we immersed ourselves in a life-style of SOPs that told us what hour to wake up in the morning, when to go to sleep at night, how to eat and drink, how to go from point A to point B, and so on.

SOPs are written standardized instructions on how to complete routine tasks ranging from minute administrative details on how to fill out forms to full instructions for combat operations. They are prepared and issued at all levels of command and carry the force of orders. Some may be very detailed, while others are as basic as those issued by Major Robert Rogers in 1759, such as "Don't forget nothing," and "Don't never take a chance you don't have to." See Annex K.

As are its other written policies and procedures, the military's SOPs are concise and logical. However, unlike other disciplines, SOPs can vary in format depending on the subject, scope, and amount of detail required. Annex J contains a full outline for an SOP. A typical SOP might include:

1. Reference to previous or related policy, if any.
2. Statement of purpose.
3. Statement of who will conform to the procedure.
4. Instructions about coordination within the organization.
5. Concise statement of how the procedure will be implemented in sequential order and, when appropriate, the rationale.

Many business functions, particularly those of an administrative nature, are routine. However, in all too many cases procedures are not only unwritten, but exist only in the minds of a few individuals. Consequently, when employees who normally handle specific responsibilities are absent, progress screeches to a halt until they return to their desks. This leads many managers to assume that some of their employees are indispensable. Although they may be loyal and trusted workers, total reliance on individuals can be dangerous to the organization. In addition to the operational hazards of such exclusive concentration of expertise, the lack of formally documented essential procedures can expose the company to the danger of being held hostage by these employees. Thus written procedures, in addition to trained backup personnel, should be required in all critical areas of operation.

A proliferation of individual fiefdoms, each having its own particular way of handling recurring tasks, is another risk large organizations cannot afford to run. It results in the development of attitudes that negatively affect the efficiency of the entire organization. The implementation of written SOPs creates unified conformity within an organization. It not only increases awareness of and adherence to internal and external procedural requirements, but allows for the transfer of employees within the company without the need for extensive retraining.

There are many different ways to prepare SOPs. Using a military format for the basic outline and giving it a business approach, we have used a document format for procedures that combines the best policies of both business and the military. In this document, policy is the general statement of a company goal, and procedures are specific chronological steps to take to reach that goal. The SOP is best kept in a loose-leaf binder to allow for changes and updates. It should be numbered by groupings or categories. Managers should assist in the preparation of the procedures and approve the final copies in order to ensure that they understand the functions to be performed by their subordinates. The procedures are to be periodically reviewed and modified as warranted by improved methods of operation and suggestions from employees.

The sample Policy and Procedure format given below outlines the disciplinary steps to be taken by management in issuing corrective and probationary warnings for misconduct by employees.

## Policy and Procedure

Date issued.
Date effective.
Title number.
Supersedes.
General subject: Personnel-supervisory management.
Title: Corrective actions.

Policy: Any employee may be warned, placed on probation, or dismissed for taking actions not in the best interest of the company. The degree and type of corrective action taken will be based upon the judgment of the employee's supervisor in accordance with company policy. Corrective action must be administered throughout the company in as uniform a manner as possible.

Procedure: Except for gross misconduct, which could require immediate dismissal, the corrective process shall consist of three progressive steps. Any employee dismissed for unsatisfactory performance of duties should normally receive no less than two warnings prior to dismissal.

1. *Corrective warning.* Corrective warnings may be oral or written, although written warnings are preferred. A copy

of all written warnings should be forwarded immediately to the personnel department for entry in the employee's personnel file. In either case, the supervisor should talk privately with the employee to cover the following points:

a. What is required of the employee and why.
b. What requirements are not being met and/or why performance is not satisfactory.
c. What corrective action is necessary.

2. *Probationary warning.* Probationary warnings should always be written. For certain serious offenses, steps one and two may be combined. A specific probationary period should be established; however, the option to lift or extend the probationary period based on future performance may be left open. A copy of the probationary warning should be forwarded to the personnel department. The supervisor should talk privately with the employee to cover the points listed above for corrective warnings. Supervisor should explain that continuation of the undesired practice could lead to employee's dismissal.

3. *Dismissal.* Prior to notifying an employee of dismissal, the immediate supervisor and his/her supervisor should prepare a written summary of the case and review all the facts with the personnel staffing manager. Copies of all documentation should be placed in the employee's personnel file immediately. When severance pay appears proper, the supervisor should consult with the director of personnel for current guidelines to determine the proper amount.

Written SOPs will not only remove the cloud of mystery that obscures particular functions within an organization, they will eliminate the need for managers to spend time providing directions for repetitive procedures. When they are well formulated and reasonably detailed, they provide a valuable contribution to the company's overall effectiveness.

# ·26·

# WRITING STYLES
## "Keep It Simple"

The military's reputation for being brutally abrupt in its written communications is consistent with its focus on clarity and brevity. Military letters tend to be devoid of descriptive adjectives and personality and are marked by a plebeian vocabulary of monosyllabic words. Bluntly they state the point to be communicated as concisely and starkly as possible. Although these general tendencies are not typically used in business, military style does drastically reduce the margin for misinterpretation and leaves little or no doubt about intentions and contents. Interestingly, it can have power and literary quality—witness U.S. Grant's memoirs, an enduring American classic of the military style.

In our first year at West Point, we were taught a basic format to follow for most written communications: state what you are going to write, write it, and then summarize what you wrote. This guideline set the foundation for classroom work and, later when we became Army officers, for organizing and writing letters and orders.

If there is one thing the military knows how to do well, it is to give orders. If, as General Patton suggested, "issuing an order is worth ten percent," then that ten percent had better be accurate and completely understood, especially in life-and-death circumstances. And the best way to be sure it is comprehensible is to adhere to the KISS adage.

This acronym, standing for "Keep It Simple, Stupid," has been around so many years that it has become something of a cliché. Yet, its merits are undeniable not only for the military, but in all endeavors. Heeding the discipline of the KISS concept, the military developed standards for written communications to provide guidelines to its members. The standards are simple, to the point, and provide criteria for composing written documents. These standards, as noted in *Manual of Common Tasks,* specify that writing should:

1. Start with a clear and concise statement of the controlling idea of the text, and the main points which support that idea. . . . Effective writing transmits a clear message in a single rapid reading, and is generally free of errors in grammar, mechanics, and usage.
2. Be compactly organized with clear transitions and effectively sequenced paragraphs, and attachments as appropriate.
3. Be clearly written in the active voice and first person, when appropriate.
4. Be concisely written without excessive jargon.
5. Exhibit correct spelling, punctuation, and grammar of standard written American English.

Along with these five basic standards, FM 101-5 provides additional guidelines to aid in the writing process. Although they are common sense, they are overlooked by just about everyone who attempts to set pencil to paper or fingers to a keyboard to transfer an idea onto a blank sheet of paper. For most of us, writing is painfully difficult regardless of our education.

1. *Unity.* Adhere to a single main issue.
2. *Accuracy.* Check facts; eliminate mechanical error.
3. *Clarity.* Write simply and clearly.
4. *Brevity.* Use simple words and short sentences. Eliminate unnecessary words and subject matters.
5. *Coherence.* Develop and arrange subject matter logically.
6. *Objectivity.* Keep an impersonal and unprejudiced viewpoint.

These six points may sound like a simplistic business writing primer; however, many managers, and even top executives, would do well to keep them in mind when composing business documents. Business letters and interoffice memos, intended to communicate important ideas, are all too often downright perplexing. Meanings are misconstrued because of poorly worded and poorly constructed sentences, and in turn numerous unnecessary problems arise that negatively affect performance, coordination, and morale. Quantity, when it comes to the written language, does not equal quality, nor does it ensure reader comprehension. On the contrary, it is often the case that the fewer the words, the more precise the content.

Several business and military executives are reputed to be harsh taskmasters when it comes to written communications. Some refuse to read documents longer than one page. Lieutenant General Gus Pagonis, the commander responsible for the movement and positioning of men, materiel, and equipment in Desert Storm, one of history's most complex logistical operations, required his subordinates to communicate with him on three-by-five-inch cards. If a request or an idea couldn't be transmitted within that space, then it hadn't been thought out thoroughly enough.

The military, in *Manual of Common Tasks*, provides a checklist to aid in the formulation and composition of written communications. The list includes commonsense ideas equally suitable for business. We recommend that this checklist be revised in business applications to include as item one: "Determine to whom the writing will be directed." Otherwise the list can be followed as it appears below, with language and supporting explanations adjusted to suit the target audience.

## Writing Performance Measures

1. Determine your purpose for writing.
2. Determine the appropriate form or type of correspondence.
3. Prepare an outline, focusing on a clear controlling idea and

major supporting points.

4. Prepare a draft which
   a. Gets the reader's attention.
   b. Clearly and quickly states your controlling idea and main supporting points.
   c. Presents your essential support in the body paragraphs, with detailed supporting material in an attachment.
   d. Provides clear transitions from introduction through conclusion.
5. Read your draft from the perspective of your audience. . . . Identify any possible confusions, misreading, ambiguities, or distracting aspects of your draft. Share your text with an associate for a similar trial response.
6. Review and revise for clarity. . . . Make sure you use the active voice and second/third person as necessary. Use familiar, plain, and accurate words. Avoid jargon, unnecessarily long words, unfamiliar acronyms, and excessive words.
7. Review and revise for compactness. Make sure you have stated your purpose/controlling idea (your specific recommendation, finding, or conclusion) up front. Make sure you clearly and logically separate your supporting text into short paragraphs or clearly titled sections. Use an executive summary or basic documentation of one or two pages, with additional supporting details in attachments, when needed.
8. Proofread for errors in correctness and format, including usage, grammar, spelling, and punctuation.

In composing business correspondence, most people mistakenly assume the reader understands what they have in mind whether it's made clear on paper or not. By taking a moment to ask a trusted employee to read the document to be certain it is comprehensible, as did Robert E. Lee prior to issuing orders, confusion and lost time at the receiving end can be reduced if not avoided altogether.

# ·27·

# BRIEFINGS
## "Brief and to the Point"

In contrast to its less than favorable reputation where writing is concerned, the military enjoys a positive reputation for its briefings. Perhaps this can to some measure be attributed to the image portrayed in Hollywood movies of handsome uniformed officers in war rooms evaluating the enemy situation and projecting how the "good guys" can win. The recent real-life military briefings on Desert Storm, televised for all the world to see, dispelled any misconceptions about the military's ability to brief as generals and colonels, attired in desert camouflage fatigues, described the unfolding of the war.

Briefing techniques are taught to all West Point cadets in classroom recitations in their first year. Standing before a blackboard, cadets learn how to explain solutions to academic problems (see Annex L for a Briefing Outline). The format is similar to West Point's guideline for writing: state what you are going to say, say it, then summarize what you said. In addition to the verbal rudiments, the cadet is trained in correct posture, making eye contact, voice projection, and the proper use of the pointer.

The academy stresses clarity, brevity, and objectivity in all briefing presentations. Performances are graded based on how well the cadet meets these standards. As with most military functions, a format, as depicted in *Manual of Common Tasks*, has been developed to aid in the preparation of briefings.

1. Determine your purpose for briefing.
2. Determine who your audience is, their current level of understanding regarding your topic, and if necessary, who the decision maker will be.
3. Determine when and where the briefing will be given, and how much time it should take.
4. Determine how much time is available for preparing the briefing.
5. Research, outline and draft the briefing text.
6. Add cues to your briefing text for visual aids and other support for your presentation.
7. Rehearse, simulating as closely as possible the audience and the actual briefing location.
8. Conduct the briefing.
9. Respond to questions.

Daily repetition of blackboard recitations increases awareness of the impact that personal appearance and body language has on how a presentation is received, regardless of the subject. Years ago in a military arts class we sat listening to a noted war hero as he stood at a podium describing a tactical maneuver on a terrain map of Germany. His attire met with Army regulations, and the left side of his chest was covered with rows of colorful ribbons representing an impressive amount of experience. However, interesting though his talk was, something about him was distracting, making it difficult to focus on the subject of his briefing. His tie was askew. His belt buckle was misaligned with his zipper seam. His name tag was crooked. So conditioned were we to be precise in all the details of our dress that these careless divergences from standards totally distracted us from his discourse.

Generals have been known to abruptly terminate briefings because the presenting officers appear overweight. We have also seen board chairmen dismiss briefers for taking too long in reaching the essential points. Too often briefings are not thoroughly planned, resulting in the speaker stepping on a virtual minefield, destroying all hope of achieving the goal. Although every executive has his or her idiosyncracies, many of these problems can be avoided by following a few basic fundamentals.

1. Recognize that your briefing is a means of communication. It is designed to inform and/or effect a decision. Your presentation should be based on what you want to accomplish. If appropriate, structure your information briefing to get a decision.

2. Preparation is key to your success. Anticipate the questions before they are asked. Conversely, do not attempt to answer a question if you do not know it; explain you will get back to them (many times people will ask a question although they already know the answer, just to catch you).

3. Be very precise and crisp in your comments. The audience will judge you accordingly.

4. Use of effective visual aids will greatly enhance your presentation. As the saying goes, a picture is worth a thousand words. But it must be accurate, meaningful, and not too busy, and must accentuate your point and be legible.

5. Flip charts, well-prepared charts, maps, slides, and overhead projectors are all effective if properly prepared and presented. However, always have a dry run to ensure the slides/charts are in proper order.

6. Pointers can be effective in noting specific portions of a chart.

7. If a podium is used, move away from it occasionally. It should not become a crutch.

8. Ascertain your position on the agenda and adapt your presentation accordingly. The longer the meeting goes on, the shorter the audience's attention span.

9. Throughout the briefing, maintain eye contact to project confidence and preparedness. Eye contact also helps to keep the attention of the audience.

Complementing these fundamentals are techniques used in conducting meetings. Routine meetings should seldom last more than one hour. They should follow prescribed agendas aimed at accomplishing the objective or with a follow-up date set by the scheduled adjournment time. If a decision is required, irrelevant discussions should be discouraged. Focus on the primary issues. When possible, material pertinent to the discussion should be distributed to the participants prior to the gathering. Adequate time should be allowed for the information to be digested and appropriate questions developed to reduce unnecessary questioning and inattention during the meeting.

Leadership plays an important role in the control, punctuality, and flow of information in meetings. It promotes open, objective participation among all parties, while forcing them to check their soap boxes at the door. Meetings should not become platforms for airing personal concerns, nor should they deteriorate into shouting debates or laboratories for committee-style compromises.

# DOCTRINES
# AND
# TACTICS

# · 28 ·

# OPERATIONAL DOCTRINES
## "Certain Fundamentals Remain Unchanged Throughout History"

In the early days of conceptualizing this book, we were initially reluctant to include tactical warfare. Most business and marketing books that attempt to draw similarities between the military and business tend to address the subject from the angle of the Principles of War (see Annex M). Consistently they state the principles, give historical examples, interlace the text with quotes from Jomini, Clausewitz, Sun Tzu, and other masters of the art, and then cite anecdotes illustrating their business applications from the annals of major corporate battles. Some of the discussions seemed so comprehensive and convincing that we began to wonder whether there was anything we could write that would not in one way or another have already been written. But the more we investigated the subject, the more apparent it became that many of the fundamental doctrines of military operations that we had studied at West Point had been partially if not totally neglected.

The curriculum on military arts and warfare at West Point is divided into two departments. One is more academic, focusing on in-depth analyses of historic campaigns and battles. When we were in these classes at West Point, we learned that most of the great commanders, such as Napoleon and Patton, were avid students of former generals and studied their strategies and tactics in order to implement them in their own campaigns. Furthermore, we learned that the fundamentals of war have remained basically unchanged throughout history, regardless of geography and the sophistication of weapons.

The second approach to the academy's military arts curriculum involves the study and on-the-ground application of tactical fundamentals. This instruction relies heavily on Army manuals such as FM 100-5, *Operations,* upon which we based this section of the book, extracting only the information that is pertinent to business warfare. The aim of the following discussions is to address the issues of how to plan for and engage with the enemy, which in the case of business is the competition. The consumer is the ultimate objective of business, but just as the military confronts enemy forces, businesses too encounter competition and must be just as knowledgeable in this regard as they are in methods to win the support of the consumer. It is of course the human dimension—sound leadership, training, and the will to fight—that is crucial in determining the outcome of any confrontation, as we have discussed in the preceding chapters.

Viewed from the perspective of Army doctrines, business consists of an enlarged battlefield extending from manufacturing plants to the ports and transportation networks to the far reaches of the marketplace. Within this area there exists a center of gravity, or the critical point from which organizations derive their strength. The center, as defined by the military, may encompass the "mass of the enemy force, a vital command and control center, its logistical base or lines of communication . . . key economic resource or locality, the strategic transport capabilities by which a nation maintains its armies in the field, or a vital part of the homeland itself."

Of course companies will not bomb their competitors' factories, lines of communication, and tactical forces, as does the military, but they will attempt to disrupt, weaken, and legally destroy their center of gravity. This center need not be physical: it may be an intangible objective, such as consumer confidence.

The center of gravity may shift as key executives are replaced, or with the introduction of new products and services, the advent of an innovative marketing approach, or a change in operation directions. Thus there must be a continual close surveillance of the competitions' organizations, financial health, access to capital, sales and marketing patterns, R & D efforts, and product strengths and weaknesses. This knowledge means that plans can be developed to marshall and concentrate superior force against a competitor's vulnerabilities and to attack.

Throughout FM 100-5's discussion on offensive operations, the word *audacious* jumps out from the pages. Although at first glance it may seem to be calling for an impetuous and perhaps unreasonable kind of risk taking, the demand for audacity makes sense, particularly if one is to confront a superior enemy. To engage in warfare is to take some severe risks. These risks involve not only human lives but the survival of nations. Temerity can prove fatal, as is true in business as well.

The Army tempers its aggressive approach with a doctrine that calls for commanders to be constantly sensitive to what are known as "culminating points." As defined by the Army, these are critical points in the offense that signify when the "balance of strength shifts from the attacking force to its opponent." At this point, the attacker "ceases to hold a significant advantage over the enemy." The offense should halt just prior to this point or risk overextension of lines of communication, exhaustion, and exposure to counterattack and defeat.

Similarly, businesses should continually monitor their progress, intelligently reallocate resources and, when appropriate, halt and regroup offensive operations when approaching their culminating points. A business plan should be developed to detail when and how to halt the offense and consolidate.

Planning for tactical operations is crucial to the outcome of any combat engagement. In the military, planning begins with the receipt of a mission, usually from a higher command. The planning process follows the guide outlined in chapter twenty-one. As stated in FM 100-5, in the execution of these plans, commanders must act "vigorously and boldly . . . to seize opportunities for decisive action," while accepting the risk of casualties and possible defeat in order to achieve their objectives. To minimize risk, plans should attempt to identify and avoid direct confrontation with the enemy's strengths. Upon this determination, all efforts should be made to attack the enemy where he is least prepared to defend.

In response to today's rapidly changing high-tech battlefields, the military advocates decentralized decision-making authority. Overcentralization, as many corporations have discovered, results in bureaucratic inertia and inhibits timely responses to tactical opportunities. Although delegating authority to subordinate commanders means running the risk of diminished precision in operations, the nature of the military battlefield and the probability of independent action dictates that authority with stated limitations be granted to the lowest practical level of command.

Businesses, under certain circumstances, can profit by decentralizing their operations. Some proponents of decentralization maintain that it makes individual units more competitive, sharper in focus, faster, and more flexible to changing situations. Furthermore, it encourages subordinates to take the initiative to confront or create opportunities that the company as a whole can exploit. Senior managers must realize, as difficult as it sometimes can be to relinquish control, that to delegate responsibility without authority is to reduce the effectiveness and motivation of managers and to discourage the development of decision-making skills in subordinates.

# ·29·

# FUNDAMENTALS OF THE OFFENSE
## "Attack Audaciously"

In the spring of 1863, when General Ulysses Grant approached the Confederate fortress at Vicksburg, Mississippi, he realized that a frontal assault on the heavily defended stronghold would be suicidal. Using feints and raids to disguise the movement of his main force, Grant boldly maneuvered around the southern flank of the Confederate defenses, cutting their lines of communication. Bewildered by the speed and daring of Grant's attack, the defending Army was rendered ineffective.

More than a century later, in 1990, the coalition forces commanded by General Norman Schwarzkopf employed a similar tactic as they swiftly moved their main forces to the western flank away from the Iraqi dug-in positions along the southern Kuwaiti border, while maintaining a mask of frontal feints, deceptions, and ruses. As in Grant's operation, the Allied mechanized units enveloped the enemy defenses and cut their lines of communication, dealing them a decisive knockout blow.

Had these tactical maneuvers not been so vigorously executed, they could have resulted in heavy losses. An alternative frontal assault would most likely have resulted in severe casualties and, in the case of Desert Storm, excited outrage in our nation, still harboring anger over Vietnam.

Although these operations, unlike those of most businesses, were carried out by large groups of men and involved vast amounts of equipment, the concentration of force against an enemy's weakness is just as vital to businesses as to the military. Small- to medium-sized companies with limited budgets tend to restrict the number of markets they target until consumer awareness and acceptance indicates a more aggressive approach is in order. This is particularly true when companies are competing against giant competitors for a market share. Attempts to take by storm the larger, more lucrative marketplaces have too often proven disastrous, particularly when those attempts are motivated by naïve egos and illusions of grandeur.

In business, warfare is not "fixed bayonets and charge," although some survivors of catastrophic encounters with competition might feel otherwise. Business *is* war, but it is played by different rules. The competition is the enemy, and often the only evidence of their presence appears at trade shows, the presence of their products in the marketplace, or in promotional ads on television and in print.

West Point taught us to attack with concentrated firepower against the enemy's soldiers, leaders, equipment, and materiel. Whenever possible, this meant we had to avoid encountering the "enemy's main strength, turn him out of his defensive positions, isolate his forces from their sources of support, and force him to fight in an unintended direction over ground he has not prepared," as stated in FM 100-5. By contrast, in business, we learned that politeness and graciousness are a stratagem one is expected to use to disguise one's enveloping assaults on a competitor's market positions. The objective is clear: to take and hold markets without suffering any unfortunate consequences.

The applicability of military offensive fundamentals to business is well demonstrated by the way in which retail shelf space is acquired and retained by product suppliers. As is true of all industries, the primary objective is to present products to potential customers. The term *shelf space* refers to the location within a retail store from which merchandise is sold in the retail marketplace.

Each industry has its own methods for selling products, and the means of distribution and the sales route taken to reach the consumer or ultimate purchaser varies with each type of product. In retail business, suppliers must convince buyers to reserve space on store shelves for their products. This can be accomplished more effectively with well-planned offensive actions.

FM 100-5 states that successful offensive actions demonstrate five major characteristics: "surprise, concentration, speed, flexibility, and audacity." Business plans should exhibit these same characteristics as well to ensure a greater chance of success. Specific steps can serve management well in developing offensive strategies and tactics to compete and win in the marketplace. These include not only gaining a detailed understanding of the competitor's situation, but also compiling an extensive dossier on buyers and purchasing agents to record their habits, patterns, likes and dislikes, and methods to reach them. Anyone who has ever made a cold first call to a buyer knows how helpful such background information can be. This is truer still when the product being sold is unfamiliar to the buyer and the competition's product has been entrenched on the store shelves for years.

Buyers for major retail chains have the power of gods and they know it. A frigid reception when one enters their offices promptly warns the lowly "peddler" to be quick and to the point. Often the seller has only one shot at convincing the buyer that his product is worthy of consideration. Like the military, where surprise as defined in FM 100-5 means "striking the enemy at a time or place, or in a manner for which he is unprepared," the seller must arouse the buyer's attention by presenting previously undisclosed sales opportunities that will increase revenues. Another effective maneuver is to find a third party known to the buyer to provide an introduction. Regardless of the tactic employed, the idea is to jolt the buyer out of his arrogance and to put the meeting into a positive light so that the merits of the products will be considered with an open mind. This requires proper prior planning and an acute concentration of effort.

Concentration, as defined by the military, means consolidating "combat power to penetrate or envelop, then shatter the enemy's defenses." The initial objective is to disarm any resistance. In business applications, this entails the formulation of an engaging, well-prepared, rehearsed presentation, where reasons for why the product should be accepted are concisely and logically cited. Marketing considerations, such as gross margins, market studies indicating consumer demands, and advertising contributions, are also effective means to penetrate a buyer's initial line of defense. Just as is true in the military, all available resources should be consolidated prior to going to battle.

Once the buyer shows signs of interest, the seller must attack swiftly. "Speed," as described in the manual, "is absolutely essential to success; it promotes surprise, keeps the enemy off balance, contributes to the security of the attacking force, and prevents the defender from taking effective countermeasures." The key is to identify and seize the moment before the buyer changes his mind, as "speed can compensate for a lack of mass (size and brand recognition) and provide the momentum necessary for attacks to achieve their aim."

The attack on the purchaser must be not only swift, but flexible. One must anticipate and formulate answers to as many questions as are likely to arise prior to the meeting. Flexibility also means being capable of immediately responding to a buyer's requests for adjustments in such areas as terms and conditions, order lead time, and shipping arrangements. The objective is to make the sale.

Audacity is perhaps the most critical, if not the most compelling, of these five traits, on both the military and business battlefields. This becomes even more crucial when the enemy or competition has distinct advantages in size and firepower. When competing against the "big boys" for shelf space, one must consider the issue of buyer and consumer loyalties. Large corporations often possess enough leverage to force buyers to reserve space for their products even though they might actually prefer to experiment with smaller suppliers who offer more attractive products and broader margins. Other buyers may decide to stick with the comfort of status quo, opting not to risk the disruption that new suppliers might create. To overcome such resistance, an offer to place merchandise on a consignment basis can be effective to demonstrate confidence by a supplier in a product's salability. Whatever the tactics employed, an aggressive yet cordial style free of obsequious innuendos can be instrumental in winning a buyer's support. As the military has stressed, "more attacks have been defeated because of lack of audacity than for any other reason."

# ·30·

# FUNDAMENTALS OF THE DEFENSE
## "The Less Decisive Form of Battle"

Once the objective has been achieved on the retail battlefield and a market has been captured, a defensive mode must be set up to protect the newly acquired terrain against outside competitors. It may also be appropriate to redirect offensive actions to improve positioning within the retail outlet. Like military terrain, shelf space location and features vary in effectiveness, with the optimum in display space being at eye level and in the most heavily trafficked sections.

The purposes of defense, as described by FM 100-5, are to repel or to defeat enemy attacks, to hold ground, to economize resources to attack elsewhere, or to buy time for reinforcements. At some point, all offensives must take on a defensive aspect, if only temporarily, in order to regroup, consolidate, resupply, and make assessment of gains and losses. Successful defensive operations, like successful offensive maneuvers, are characterized by specific features: preparation, disruption, concentration, and flexibility.

Preparation, as FM 100-5 details, involves "positioning forces in depth, war-gaming plans, organizing the force of movement and support, mounting reconnaissance and surveillance operations forward of the defended area. . . ." Applying this to a retail business scenario, the defender should rapidly undertake a multitude of activities to ensure favorable product positioning on store shelves, with long-term objectives to seize the most optimal locations within stores. A number of steps should be taken to strengthen one's defensive position.

First, never allow the amount of merchandise in the store to fall too low or to go out of stock. This may be comparable to thinly protected defensive lines on the military battlefield. Secondly, the hard-earned victories and rapport won with store managers and buyers can be placed at a precarious risk if shelves become bare as a result of suppliers' failure to fulfill orders in a timely manner. Periodically introduce new products to keep your image fresh and exciting, and make service and detailing visits on a regular basis with store operations and key people. Warm and trustworthy relations with buyers and managers build a major stronghold to defend positioning or shelf space from a competitor's attacks.

As does the military, defenders should continually reconnoiter competitors' activities in the marketplace. This may include examining their pricing, the variety and quality of products, new product introductions, new products in the R & D pipeline, advertising and promotional efforts, patterns of market expansion or contraction, changes in methods of sales and distribution, reputations of and changes in key managers, financial conditions, timeliness of replenishment of inventory, new factories and locations, and other considerations as well, as noted in chapter eighteen. Analysis of this intelligence is vital to management's anticipation of the ifs, whens, and hows of future attacks.

The defender should never wait for competition to strike. The full range of the competitor's possible courses of action must be contemplated. Ask repeatedly "What if this happens?" and develop contingency plans to confront all probable offensive actions. Flanking attacks made through purchasing agents are to be expected. These assaults will attempt to create the impression that the competitors' products are superior in quality, performance, profitability, and service support. However, the advantage usually rests with the defender who is a known entity to the buyer. If such attacks persist, the defender will eventually need to take the initiative to quiet the competition by disruptive tactics.

Disruptive operations on the military battlefield do not generally exhibit the subtlety of those in business. As noted in FM 100-5, military operations involve the disarrangement of the enemy's synchronization of operations "by separating his forces; by interrupting his fire support, logistical support, or command and control; by breaking the tempo of his operation; or by ruining the coordination of enemy combined and supporting arms." Of course it is not only improbable but would be ill-advised for a business to physically sabotage a competitor's manufacturing operations, warehouses, lines of distribution and sales networks. However, other measures can be employed to disrupt their efforts to regain or take shelf space, such as maintaining close coordination with buyers and store managers and strategically placing ads to preempt competitive activity.

To formulate an effective defense, intelligence on the enemy must be gathered and analyzed. It should indicate when the attack is to begin and with what intensity. The ability to anticipate ad campaigns, new product introductions, price reductions, and other tactical moves will allow the defender time to concentrate forces to preempt such maneuvers and minimize or totally block them. FM 100-5 states, "Effective reconnaissance and security forces are vital to give the tactical commander time to discern the form of the attack and to concentrate forces and fires against it."

A properly implemented intelligence program will reveal the concentration or massing of competitive resources, including talent and capital. Early detection can destroy the elements of surprise and initiative critical to the enemy's offense against fortified defensive positions. For example, initiating an ad campaign prior to the competition can dilute its impact. This kind of maneuver makes similar competitive actions appear to be nothing but a case of monkey see, monkey do, and it diminishes their image in the buyers' and consumers' eyes. Timing and the degree of implementation must be prudently considered prior to promotional commitments, and the costs for advertising and new product development and introductions must be assessed. For companies with small advertising budgets, it is unlikely that direct attacks on competitive products will be made through the media. Negative assaults are risky under the best conditions and often backfire when inadequate capital is available to bankroll the high cost of necessary propaganda. If a company opts for the tactic of price slashing as a defense, it should be remembered that reduced profit margins can seriously affect the company's viability.

It is rarely possible to achieve the ideal of always anticipating the competition's intentions. The defenders, FM 100-5 states, should therefore be prepared to "counter or evade the attacker's blow, then strike back effectively." To a large extent this can be achieved in the planning phases, by developing contingency responses to a multitude of likely offensive actions by competitors. Such preparation might include setting aside capital as reserves for such an occasion. The objective is to have, FM 100-5 goes on to detail, the flexibility to "respond to the crisis and pass quickly to the attack whenever the opportunity arises." As is true in military battles, the defender must never forget that the aggressor decides when and where they will attack.

The concept outlined in chapter eighteen, the Estimate of the Situation, is appropriate for formulating a defense plan. As FM 100-5 instructs, it should be based on "locating, containing, and defeating the attacker's main and supporting efforts . . . making use of every resource available to offset the attacker's numerical advantage, to identify dangerous threats, and to mass combat power against the vulnerabilities of the enemy force." Communication must remain continually open with buyers, who must be reassured of a commitment to their best interests, which means satisfying customer demands, maximizing shelf space, and increasing sales.

Unlike the military, where time can be critical in organizing defensive measures because of the rapid flux of changes on the battlefield, businesses usually have adequate time to prepare for anticipated attacks. Still, it is wisest to maintain at all times contingency arrangements to counter surprise competitive assaults.

# ·31·

# PERSONAL COUNTERATTACK
## "Take Action to Regain the Initiative"

America's military and corporations are undergoing massive build-downs in sweeping efforts to cut costs and make organizations profitably competitive. En masse, individuals are suddenly finding themselves out on the street confronting the challenge of finding comparable paying jobs. The demoralizing, shell-shocked sensation of losing employment can be likened to the way soldiers feel when under heavy enemy mortar attack. A sense of helplessness and an inclination to wallow in self-pity pervades. Such listlessness on the military battlefield almost guarantees annihilation by the enemy.

The military teaches that action is the remedy to overcome paralysis induced by severe losses. After an enemy attack, the commander immediately consolidates his unit and assesses the situation. Firepower and soldiers are promptly reorganized to repel future assaults. The goal is to create an environment that will allow a resumption of offensive tactics. In order to minimize chaos following an enemy attack, the military stipulates that when time permits counterattack plans are to be prepared and rehearsed. Since these plans are based on anticipated enemy actions, assumptions are a critical part of the process.

Counterattack, as defined by the military, is an "attack by part or all of a defending force against an enemy attacking force, for such specific purposes as regaining ground lost or cutting off or

151

destroying enemy advance units, with the general objective of denying the enemy the attainment of his purpose in attacking." To assist commanders and staff in planning for counterattacks, the military provides the following checklist.

1. Plan for the worst case first.
2. Do you need to contain the penetration before committing the counterattack?
3. Do we have the right forces for the situation? If not, can we get them from higher?
4. Is there sufficient fire support available and planned?
5. What are the logistical support requirements and are they available?
6. Does the route for the counterattack force provide ease of movement, cover, and concealment?
7. Keep the plan simple.
8. Ensure that everyone is aware of the action.

Timing of the counterattack is particularly critical, since a portion or all of the reserves are committed, leaving the unit precariously vulnerable. Reserves are considered pivotal to the counterattack, and the military prescribes that commanders of larger units keep at least one-third of their maneuver forces in reserve. Reserves should likewise be part of business strategies, be they cash or other assets that can strengthen counteractions or buy time if deemed appropriate.

At the personal level, actions taken by individuals who have suffered setbacks can be similar to those taken by a military commander after sustaining an enemy attack. By anticipating the possibility of business loss or job termination, contingency plans can be prepared and, when needed, implemented without waste of time and undue distress. A carefully thought out plan devised under calm, controlled conditions will lessen emotional trauma and provide objectively designed courses of action. It should require proactive measures to regain inner balance and a sense of doing something constructive, with the objective of maintaining a positive mental attitude during the initial period of psychological adjustment.

Unfortunately, many people live from paycheck to paycheck and do not plan for loss of work. Suddenly faced with mortgage, medical, and cost of living expenses without income, one's immediate tendency is to withdraw. This is like standing in a mine field under intense hostile fire. To do nothing is lethal!

Business is war, and the fight to regain the initiative can be extremely taxing to personal strength. Psychological warfare demands that one keep a cool head during the onslaught of financial worries. The unfairness of former employers should not be dwelled on. The enemies are rejection, inadequacy, denial, and helplessness, all of which are positioned in one's head. These depressant invaders must be aggressively attacked and destroyed before they penetrate too deeply into the psyche and kill self-esteem and confidence. As with the military counterattack, an offensive environment must be established. The adage that the "best defense is a good offense" is most appropriate. Opportunity does not come out of nowhere; one must seek it.

# ·32·

# HOSTILE TAKEOVERS
## "Develop Action Plans Before They Are Needed"

As competition in business builds in intensity, it can expand into a full-fledged war. Realizing he must proceed audaciously to avoid being repelled or defeated by violent counterattacks, the attacker must also understand that a defender will commit his entire reserves rather than surrender to and, in the worst-case scenario, merge forces with a more powerful entity, a "white knight." This kind of business warfare resembles classic military operations and describes one of the business world's most intense and combative engagements: hostile takeovers.

Many of the military fundamentals taught at West Point and techniques discussed in earlier chapters can be applied to formulate strategies and tactics either to attack a potential acquisition target or to defend against unwanted advances. In either case, action plans should be developed and rehearsed before they are needed.

The term *hostile takeover* refers to an unfriendly effort by an aggressor to conquer and take possession of the assets of a defender who does not want to be taken over. Usually, the aggressor force is larger, has more resources, and has selected an acquisition target in order to grow still larger, to fatten its earnings per share, for synergistic reasons such as the broadening of its product base and distribution system, or to eliminate competition. In this chapter we will examine the subject from two points of view: the aggressor's and the defender's.

■ ■ ■

*Aggressor:* The initial phase of an acquisition program should follow the Staff Study format to determine the appropriateness and timing of an acquisition, identify and qualify an acquisition target, and select the type of transaction that would prove most beneficial to the acquiring company. This will answer the who, what, where, when, how, and why of the attack. Before commencing with any hostile action, a friendly offer should first be extended to the targeted company. If such offers are rejected, the aggressor then must consider the costs and benefits of an antagonistic approach. In light of the potential consequences of such an endeavor, the CEO should orchestrate and be the signature officer to all of the operation's critical elements.

Once the analysis is complete and the targeted company selected, the aggressor should follow the format of the Intelligence Estimate to obtain as much information as possible about the proposed target. Of particular importance in this phase is a thorough analysis of the fundamental reasons for a takeover attempt and the targeted company's strengths, weaknesses, compatibilities, and differences. Much of this intelligence can be gathered by close examination of their products (existing and future), R & D efforts, marketplace, market shares, financial condition, current and projected earnings, management, labor skills, union contracts, facilities, distribution network, sales force, legal proceedings, type of stock, likely "white knights" based on known relationships, and other visible and invisible assets and liabilities. Understanding the enemy is essential. Surprises resulting from inadequate investigation can prove costly and even fatal to businesses in this type of warfare. In instances where intelligence is inadequate or missing, assumptions should be carefully developed, weighed, and assiduously cross-examined for inclusion in the decision-making model.

If the findings of the Intelligence Estimate show sufficient cause to proceed, the aggressor should prepare a detailed analysis of all factors affecting the attack, using the Commander's Estimate format. This combines validated and assumed enemy intelligence and battlefield conditions to create models that concentrate on the most probable courses of action. Rumors, misleading press reports, arbitrageurs' manipulations, and secondary targets should not distract the aggressor from focusing on the objectives. From these conclusions, an Operations Plan can be constructed to guide the offensive forces in their execution.

Secrecy during the entire analysis and planning phase is absolutely critical. The element of surprise often proves pivotal to an operation's success. This means that only those who have a need to know should have knowledge of the company's intentions, although individuals critical to the operation's success should be included in the plan's development. Just as supplies and troops must be positioned prior to a battle, necessary support elements such as investment bankers, attorneys, accountants, and proxy solicitors should be brought in to contribute their expertise from the early stages. After the plan has been completed, war gamed, and deemed ready, the CEO initiates the plan into an Attack Order.

The attack must be vigorous and unrelenting. The use of feints and ruses, where appropriate, allows for the concentration of forces at the enemy's weakest points, permitting a bold ultimate move that will catch the targeted company off guard and unprepared to defend itself. A feint or ruse may involve cleverly worded press releases, unsubstantiated legal proceedings, and planted rumors. The attack must be tightly controlled throughout the maneuver to ensure that the advancing forces do not overrun the objective and to preclude the possibility of the combatants becoming so involved in the battle that it becomes an emotional issue, resulting in an overpayment for the acquisition.

*Defender:* The analysis and planning methods used in the offense are equally applicable to the development of a tenacious defensive strategy. Although some companies, having no plans, knowledge, or fortitude for a traumatic and costly fight, will immediately succumb to overpowering threats, others realize that to resist may be to risk everything, including the company's total assets, in order to ward off the aggressors. During the defense, management of a publicly held corporation should take into consideration the best interests of its shareholders and how to maximize their stock value, regardless of the consequences to their own personal positions or future.

If a company decides to defend itself aggressively, the Staff Study and Estimate of the Situation provide comprehensive guidelines for understanding possible attacks, potential enemies, and alternative defensive tactics. It points out the several techniques available to counter the attack, which should be examined as to their efficacy against various offensive maneuvers and which should be incorporated in the plan prior to any enemy incursions.

Preliminary military defensive measures involve erecting defensive perimeters, laying mines, and the setting of fields of fire. The business version of such measures might entail, among other possibilities, instituting corporate charter and by-law changes that allow for staggered board terms, "supermajority" voting requirements, special-meeting call requirements, change of control provisions in management employment agreements, "self-tender" of the stock, conversion of preferred stock, increasing the company's debt, and recruitment of a "white knight." Regardless of the technique, the defender should hit the aggressor hard and make him pay dearly each time he attempts to encroach on the defender's territory. The defender must keep in mind the fact that the attacker is likewise cognizant of these various measures and is likely to design his strategy to circumvent them.

As the enemy draws nearer, legal barrages can be fired to slow and impede progress of the attacking forces. The company's production, sales, and marketing efforts must be optimized in order to retain the support of loyal stockholders. The enemy is likely to bombard shareholders with propaganda in an attempt to discredit current management and board members and extoll the benefits of their own proposal. Initially putting forth a "Saturday night special" or a "straight tender offer" inducement to cross over to the enemy's lines, the enemy may follow with a "two-tiered" offer in which an attractive price for shares is established to gain a controlling interest in the company. Subsequent offers for the balance of shares is normally tendered at a lower price. This can severely test the shareholders' allegiance to the existing regime. Such methods of creating constant financial pressure demands that management reassure both shareholders and employees that all efforts are being taken to protect their interests. Continual open communication with employees and shareholders is crucial to the maintenance of a unified defensive front. The troops must be kept informed so that they don't read it first in the newspapers.

The most important element of either an attack or defense in a hostile takeover is the commitment and tenacity of senior management. They must lead by example, convince the employees and shareholders that they are concerned about their best interests, keep them informed of the progress of the fight, and constantly remain visible.

# ·33·

# INVASION OF FOREIGN MARKETS
## "Costly Pitfalls and Legal Entanglements"

Standing on an airstrip waiting to board a jet that would transport us across the Pacific to Southeast Asia, we wondered what lay in store for us and whether we would ever see America again. Four years at West Point followed by military schooling had trained us for war. However, we had been trained in World War II tactics designed to fight Soviet armored divisions in Europe and on the Russian steppes, not pajama-clad guerrillas hiding in jungles and villages among Vietnamese peasants.

The lessons we learned in Vietnam have remained with us throughout our business careers. Having learned never to presume that the strategies, tactics, and weapons that are successful on one battlefield are automatically appropriate for another, we have tempered eagerness to expand into foreign markets with well-founded caution. Our military experiences confirmed the necessity of thoroughly understanding the terrain and the enemy prior to initiating offensive operations. Similarly, businesses must comprehend the foreign marketplace, the competition and, most importantly, the consumer prior to entering new markets.

The Estimate of the Situation formats outlined in previous chapters provide management with checklists to collect and analyze intelligence in order to address these issues. From such analysis, product, market, and distribution strategies can be developed to meet the demands of distant markets and consumers, and arrange for the positioning of products and people prior to the commencement of sales.

Although this may seem to be mere common sense, even giant industrial powers with access to the brightest people and state-of-the-art computers have botched opportunities and lost major battles because they failed to comprehend and anticipate what was in store for them on foreign turf. Had America's automobile manufacturers heeded the evaluation of the intelligence gathered in their own estimates, they certainly would not have attempted to sell large, gas-guzzling left-hand drive cars to Japan, where roads are narrow and all Japanese cars are right-hand drive. Clearly this would be a tough sell had there been an open-door policy toward American automobile imports.

Similarly, foreign beverage manufacturers have failed to establish a market presence in the United States because they are unable to appeal to the American taste. Compounding the difficulties of meeting the needs of an extremely sophisticated consumer, foreign companies must also overcome their perception of the United States marketplace as a jungle filled with costly pitfalls and legal entanglements. The horror stories of those who have attempted to cross its shores serve as an effective embargo of intimidation for others who aspire to enter the world's largest and most lucrative consumer market. A nightmarish conception prevails of armies of attorneys with their sights set on unsuspecting foreigners and armed with "trumped-up" product liability claims. Exacerbating these litigation worries is the dilemma of how to abide by all of the many and varied requirements of each and every federal, state, and municipality regulatory agency in this consumer-protected economy, not to mention the high costs of entry and the intense competition.

It is understandable that many foreign companies feel reluctant to enter the United States, particularly since they often lack a "feel" for the American marketplace, its idiosyncracies, its diverse culture, and the unpredictability of its consumers. Such ventures can indeed seem like a military expedition into an unfamiliar jungle, and certainly no such venture should be embarked upon without a map—a business plan—that clearly defines the terrain.

Just as United States companies must assess foreign markets prior to investing large sums of capital, international firms should develop their own decision papers before entering the United States. This often requires the assistance of a professional experienced in the ins and outs of the American marketplace. Since most business decisions inevitably revolve around profitability, the professional should develop premises and assumptions that realistically portray existing and future market conditions and anticipated consumer demands. Regrettably, many foreign companies attempt to transplant premises and assumptions valid in their own country across economic borders without considering the differences between their culture and that of the United States. This can mean the venture is doomed before it is even truly begun, and it perpetuates the reputation of the American marketplace as being a jungle.

The business plan should be the primary document from which decisions are made regarding entry into foreign markets. It identifies risks, potential profit, and when appropriate, explains why the project should be aborted. It also addresses sources of intimidation with the intent of destroying myths. Caution is to be used in assessing the ability of a professional before commissioning one to assist in developing such a plan. Many large consulting firms tend to inundate their clients with reams of unnecessary printed matter such as U.S. Commerce reports, and so on. Too often these mountains of documents have no bearing on the critical path necessary to arrive at economically sound decisions. The number of pages included in a plan is not an indication of its validity or usefulness. Similarly, the necessity for quantitative research studies and focus group sessions should be questioned, since often a more savvy adviser may deem them an untimely and unneeded expenditure of capital.

Once a decision has been made to proceed to the next stage of expansion, a practice profitably employed by many Japanese companies may prove crucial to overcoming United States market resistance. The hiring of an American guide to provide professional services to effect the preparation of a plan can be a tremendous help. The selection of a guide is often influenced by simple human chemistry, but the professional should have a keen sense for shifting trends, future consumer needs, and market, economic, and political conditions. Combined with the business plan to serve as a map, the assistance of a guide can help lift the embargo of intimidations, boost confidence, and make the journey both profitable and fun.

# ·34·

# WAR GAMES
## "Exposes Potential Holes in Plans Before the Action Begins"

Fundamentals of offense and defense tactics have been time-tested over centuries on battlefields around the globe. Despite the modernization of today's weapons and electronics, the principles of warfare remain the same as they ever were. As mentioned earlier, these principles exist in print and are available for study by anyone, including adversaries. America's military actions and reactions can be anticipated based on these fundamentals. While this might suggest opponents enjoy a distinct advantage, as in the game of chess, knowing the classic moves and understanding the opposition's mentality does not guarantee checkmate. In the course of combat, the battlefield can change in complexion any number of times, momentarily revealing weaknesses and opportunities that are not necessarily apparent on paper.

In order to expose potential holes in plans, when time permits, commanders war game operations prior to entering the real battlefield. We were first introduced to war gaming as plebes in military tactics. We brainstormed tactical courses of action to take or hold objectives and simulated battle areas in sandboxes by sculpting hills, valleys, and streams out of sand to create models of actual terrain. The miniaturized battlefield with enemy positions depicted by pebbles and twigs gave us a bird's eye view and graphically demonstrated the areas we were later to encounter.

In Vietnam, we formed similar models out of mud and loose dirt. On one occasion we were informed by intelligence that enemy radio signals had been emitted from an area where a tiny island was located in the middle of a large marsh. The island was the most likely position of transmission, and because of the clear visibility the flat marshlands afforded the enemy, we decided to conduct a surprise night raid under the cover of darkness. The island, as indicated on our map, was about the size of an oval-shaped football field and surrounded by an armpit-deep swamp. Using an aerial photograph as a guide, in the dirt next to our foxhole we molded the features of the island terrain and its surrounding marshes. This allowed us to envision a variety of approach routes to the objective, as well as alternate escape routes, rendezvous points, and positions for security and protective fires. We could see the elevated banks where our troops would rise out of the swamp and assault the Vietcong we hoped would be sleeping as flares lit up the sky like daylight. Continuing to advance across the mound of dirt, we would complete a sweeping tactical maneuver that would destroy the enemy.

Thus we could picture the entire operation from the beginning to the end. Numerous possible contingencies and reactions to various enemy responses were contemplated, and our knowledge of the area and what to expect was substantially increased, enabling us to slip into the water and attack with a confidence rather than in the grip of complete uncertainty.

Subsequently, at a corps headquarter that commanded over a hundred thousand troops, we observed similar types of war games conducted on a grander scale. In a large war room, a massive terrain map of the corps' area of operation depicted allied and enemy troop positions. The corps commander, key staff officers, and subordinate division and air support commanders brainstormed alternative courses of action to engage and defeat the enemy, following the analysis of courses of action noted in the Commander's Estimate of the Situation (see Annex D). As though playing chess on a giant board, they debated the advantages and disadvantages of a variety of maneuvers until a decision could be made. These overall strategies created a blueprint for tactical operations that spanned the hierarchy from the top down to the company and platoons.

Today high-tech computers are used to accomplish the same basic war gaming activities. Minor skirmishes to major wars are now designed, formatted, and played to determine the most likely scenario and most favorable plan of action. As in all military plans and operations, known facts and established parameters provide the framework for the model. Just as critical to the effectiveness of these electronic exercises is the development of assumptions that articulate the strengths, weaknesses, and predictable actions and reactions of opposing forces. Such computerized war games were played prior to Operation Desert Storm, allowing commanders to weigh potential problems and opportunities before the air and ground forces were committed.

War game methodology can be equally effective in business applications. Like the sandbox technique used by the military, prototype models and schematic layouts add a third dimension to the problem-solving process. It is always much easier to understand a concept if one can visualize it.

For example, while working with retail chains expanding outlets into new locations, we drew concentric circles on a road map around proposed new sites indicating demographics, consumer buying patterns, moving and walking traffic counts, distance to distribution routes, and print, radio, and television media support. Complementing this diagram were financial models that forecasted consumer demands and related costs to reach potential shoppers.

For strategic planning, war gaming is an invaluable tool. As in the military, modeling and simulation creates a realistic visualization of the business battlefield and the consequences of changes in the economy and other major factors. Furthermore, it encourages managers to anticipate alternative courses of action that might be required by the advent of new competing products and increased interest rates. Essential to such programs is the active participation of the CEO and all key managers within an organization. The model should not be designed and manipulated solely by "number crunchers." Facts, parameters, and assumptions established should include those of appropriate managers. As is true of virtually any plan, reasonable and valid assumptions are crucial to the effectiveness of the model.

165

Similar to the way a sandbox is used to depict military objectives, a financial model should reflect the financial goals of the business. Businesses typically use a balance sheet and income and cash flow statements to view their structural foundation. Detailed items are divided into categories, such as advertising and salary expenses. Depending on the size of the organization, the method for computing data varies. Large corporations may utilize multiple mainframes capable of merging data from peripheral computers located throughout the world. Sophisticated spread sheet software provides rapid and consistent computation. But in some cases, a piece of paper, a pencil, and a calculator are all one needs to be able to understand the impact of changing financial conditions. Regardless of the kind of equipment used, the method to be employed follows a standard sequence: set the structure, collect current and historical data, create and adjust assumptions, formulate and analyze projections of various possible scenarios, and refine.

As noted in earlier chapters covering the business plan and the development of assumptions, accuracy in the premises and assumptions based on crucial factors such as anticipated sales and expense trends is imperative for a model to be effective. Along with historical data, they form the basis for the pro forma balance sheet and earnings and cash flow statements. War gaming these numbers and their underlying rationale should not be merely an exercise confined to an accountant's computer monitor. Management as a team should participate and contribute to evaluating probabilities. Vigorous discussions should ensue to challenge assumptions and projections and to inspire new and innovative approaches. Not only will this process help to paint a clearer picture of the future, it will help line managers to become intimately involved in the development of plans and to understand what will be required of them to achieve objectives.

Whether it is done by a simple, on-the-spot sketch in the dirt or by means of highly sophisticated computer modeling, war gaming is critical to the success of any organization, be it military or business. It allows leaders to visualize the confrontation, its problems and risks, and its opportunities—before the real action begins.

# ·35·

## CONCLUSION
### "Business Is War"

Business strategies and tactics are highly reminiscent of those employed on the military battlefield. Many CEOs look upon themselves as generals in command of corporate armies, and often they proclaim that business is war. Indeed, when we first made the transition from the military into corporate America, we often felt as though we had merely changed uniforms. Only the language seemed unfamiliar.

If it is true that business is war, certainly businesses would do well to learn from professionals trained in warfare. Success on the battlefield, as West Point teaches all its cadets, is not achieved solely through decisive tactical ability but requires a solid foundation of training, discipline, and leadership. These time-tested fundamentals are equally crucial to success in business. Offensive and defensive maneuvers clearly are essential elements of business operations, but without well-planned, organized, coordinated, and timely executed tasks on all operational levels, they are rendered virtually ineffective.

Founded in 1802, West Point has consistently been America's source of military leaders. West Point's building blocks of fundamentals create a broad foundation within its cadets, starting with the simple left foot principle and continuing with increasingly more advanced concepts. Character is the glue that holds the blocks firmly in place, and certainly the West Point immersion model would fail in accomplishing its mission to develop leaders if it did not stress the absolute imperative of maintaining integrity.

In recent years, America's businesses have lost their cohesion and competitive edge, dismissing long-range goals and yielding to short-term financial pressures. Some critics contend that the nation has lost its work ethic. The public has grown undeniably skeptical about certain American-made products and extremely doubtful about corporate management's veracity and strength of character. The results of this situation are reflected in the marketplace, where foreign competition has beaten America's production forces on its own turf, providing reasonably priced products to a consumer who is more quality conscious than loyal to origin of manufacture.

This loss of ground was not necessary, nor is it irreparable. However, to regain strength, businesses must return to the fundamentals that made them the world's dominant industrial power. Leadership, discipline, high ethical standards, and investments in the distant future should become paramount priorities. Given that America's systematic problems are deeply rooted, the return to basics demands standardized systems, procedures, and decision-making models to hold management's focus on the mission and strategic objectives.

Lean, mean, and to the point, the techniques and formats taught at West Point and outlined in this book are specifically designed to create the discipline required to stay within well-defined guidelines. They leave little room for misinterpretation, and their logical sequencing leads directly to sound conclusions without wasting time. These techniques provide a no-nonsense approach to problem solving that can save lives, win wars, and applied to corporate situations, can contribute significantly to business victories.

While the various military methodologies provide guidelines from which management can develop or modify their own practices, it is in the adoption of its fundamental philosophies that business can benefit most from the military. Many businesses are lacking in leadership and ethics, two qualities that West Point has been devoted to developing in its cadets for nearly two centuries.

Successful leadership requires that subordinates feel a sense of trust in their leader. Without trust, subordinates are reluctant to follow and may be inclined to jump ship at the first opportunity. Trust means believing in another person's ability and, more importantly, his or her sense of fairness and integrity.

West Point teaches that leadership demands a constant awareness of human behavior, including one's own as well as that of others. Cadets are taught to lead by example, which can mean digging one's own foxhole even when one could issue a simple command to demand that a soldier of lower rank do it. Leading by example sends a powerful message to the tens and hundreds of soldiers under one's command. Not only does it boost their confidence and the esprit de corps, it builds character within the leader.

Having been students ourselves of the sound leadership principles taught in the military and recognizing their positive impact on subordinates, we are continually dismayed at the pervasive absence of this quality throughout the business world. All too often corporate executives remain confined to their suites and seldom wander among their employees. The motivational energy that leaders inspire in their men on the military battlefields is sorely lacking in today's business environment. It is difficult to imagine how executives responsible for directing corporations can be effective leaders without human contact. Wars are not won by fax machines and interoffice memos. They are won, in the military and in business, by leaders leading.

The leaders who served as role models for both of us each possessed a sensitivity to the individual needs, capabilities, and aspirations of their subordinates. This sensitivity by no means implied a softness or meant that demands on us were less exacting. On the contrary, it often meant pushing us to go beyond our perceived limitations, often to our dislike at the time, although we always respected the demands to achieve more. Our respect was built on the knowledge that the leader's first and foremost concern was the welfare and morale of the subordinates.

Looking back, it is clear that each of our mentors upheld a code of honor demanding that regardless of the physical and financial pressures, one must not succumb to the temptation of quick profit or to avoid eminent personal loss. Although some of these mentors were not graduates of the academy, each ascribed to the three pillars for which West Point stands: Duty, Honor, Country. Their sense of duty, not only to the task and to the country but to their subordinates, inspired in us an unwavering loyalty, lifted our self-esteem, and boosted our will to accomplish our jobs to the best of our abilities. Without question, we would have followed them anywhere, even into the depths of hell.

By adopting this commitment to fundamentals, business executives, workers, and ultimately America's companies, like its military, will regain their worldwide preeminence and respect. *Duty, Honor, Company* serves well as a motto and as a way of life for business success.

# ★ IV ★

# ANNEXES

# ANNEX A

# MISSION DIRECTIVE TO GENERAL EISENHOWER

12 February 1944

1. You are hereby designated as Supreme Allied Commander of the forces placed under your orders for operations for liberation of Europe from Germany. Your title will be Supreme Commander Allied Expeditionary Forces.

2. Task. You will enter the continent of Europe and, with the other United Nations, undertake operations aimed at the heart of Germany and the destruction of her armed forces. The date for entering the Continent is the month of May, 1944. After adequate Channel ports have been secured, exploitation will be directed towards securing an area that will facilitate both ground and air operations against the enemy.

3. Notwithstanding the target above, you will be prepared at any time to take immediate advantage of favorable circumstances, such as withdrawal by the enemy on your front to effect a reentry into the Continent with such forces as you have available at the time. A general plan for this operation when approved will be furnished for your assistance.

4. Command. You are responsible to the Combined Chiefs of Staff and will exercise command generally in accordance with

the diagram in Appendix (attached). Direct communication with the United States and British Chiefs of Staff is authorized in the interest of facilitating your operations and for arranging necessary logistic support.

5. Logistics. In the United Kingdom, the responsibility for logistics organization, concentration, movement, and supply of forces to meet the requirements of your plan will rest with British Service Ministries so far as British Forces are concerned. So far as the United States Forces are concerned, this responsibility will rest with the United States War and Navy Departments. You will be responsible for the coordination of logistical arrangements on the Continent. You will be responsible for coordinating the requirements of British and United States forces under your command.

6. Coordination of operations of other Forces and Agencies. In preparation for your assault on enemy-occupied Europe, sea and air forces, agencies of sabotage, subversion, and propaganda acting under a variety of authorities, are now in action. You may recommend any variation in these activities which may seem desirable to you.

7. Relationship to United Nations Forces in other areas. Responsibility will rest with the Combined Chiefs of Staff for resupplying information relating to operations of the Forces of the USSR for your guidance in timing your operations. It is understood that the Soviet Forces will launch an offensive at about the same time as OVERLORD with object of preventing the German forces from transferring from the Eastern to the Western front. The Allied Commander-in-Chief, Mediterranean Theater, will conduct operations designed to assist your operation, including the launching of an attack against the south of France at about the same time as OVERLORD. The scope and timing of his operations will be decided by the Combined Chiefs of Staff. You will establish contact with him and submit to the Combined Chiefs of Staff your views and recommendations regarding operations from the Mediterranean in support of your attack from the United Kingdom. The combined Chiefs of Staff will place under your command the forces operating in

southern France as soon as you are in a position to assume such command. You will submit timely recommendations compatible with this regard.

8. Relationship with Allied Governments—the establishment of Civil Governments in Liberated Allied Territories and the administration of enemy territories. Further instructions will be issued to you on these subjects at a later date.

Source: Department of the Army. FM 101-5, *Staff Organization and Operations.*

# ANNEX B

# DECISION-MAKING SEQUENCE

1. A higher headquarters normally assigns the mission (step 1), but the commander may develop or deduce the mission. The commander may initiate his mission analysis at this point. Mission analysis is discussed in paragraph 3 below.
2. The commander's staff provides the commander with the information available (step 2). Subordinate commanders receive information concerning the mission and the situation as early as practical in the planning phase and at least by the time staff estimates are being prepared.
3. Based on this information, the commander completes the mission analysis and issues planning guidance (step 3).
   a. The purpose of the mission analysis is to ensure that the commander fully understands the mission and to allow him to develop the tasks essential to the accomplishment of the mission. The commander performs his mission analysis by identifying the specified and implied tasks contained in his mission.
      (1) Specified tasks are those tasks delineated in the mission received from higher headquarters or the missions developed or deduced by the commander.
      (2) Implied tasks are those additional tasks that the commander identifies as essential to ensure accomplishment of the mission. When identifying implied tasks, the commander should exercise caution not to include tasks that are routine or inherent in the mission.

(3) Besides identifying the specified and implied tasks, the commander may elect to reword one or more of the specified tasks given him by a higher headquarters.

b. The mission analysis results in the commander's guidance to his staff members for use in preparing or revising their estimates. The amount of planning guidance varies with each mission, the volume and validity of information available, the situation, and the experience of the commander and the staff. Planning guidance is not limited to one specific step in the sequence of actions. However, initial guidance should precede the preparation of staff estimates.

(1) The commander normally includes in his initial guidance his restated mission as determined by his mission analysis; his general plan for using nuclear and chemical weapons, if appropriate; his considerations for the possible use of tactical cover and deception and any other factors that he considers important at this time; and any courses of action that he wishes developed.

(2) Unless higher headquarters has directed a specific course of action, the commander does not select the course of action at this time because to do so would prevent objective and unbiased staff estimates.

4. The commander's restated mission becomes paragraph 1 of all staff estimates. Based on the restated mission and planning guidance received, the coordinating staff officers prepare their staff estimates (step 4), assisted by special staff officers, who may also prepare their own estimates if necessary. The coordinating staff officers present their estimates to the commander, which results in recommendations on the actions that the commander should take to accomplish his mission.

5. Following the decision statement (the last step of the commander's estimate), the commander may provide the staff with his overall concept of how the operation will be conducted (commander's concept), which is an amplification of his decision and explains any aspects he considers necessary.

6. A careful analysis, based on a complete understanding of the decision and the commander's concept of the operation, leads to a determination by all staff members of the actions required by the commander to carry the operation to successful completion and to preparation of plans or orders (step 6).

7. The staff normally submits plans and orders to the commander

for approval (step 7) before they are published as plans or orders (step 8). (Step 7 may be omitted if the urgency of the situation so warrants and if the commander has delegated such authority).

8. Command and staff supervision of the execution of orders (step 9) is a continuing action, based on the commander's decision and his concept of the operation.

Source: Department of the Army. FM 101-5, *Staff Organization and Operations.*

# ANNEX C

# STAFF STUDY

Subject: Training Program

1. *Problem.* To develop a training technique to sustain the ability of the support element to provide efficient, responsive support.
2. *Assumptions.*
   a. Training time and resources will be available to support a sustained training program.
   b. A recurring training program will improve the efficiency and responsiveness of the support elements to mission requirements.
3. *Facts bearing on the problem.*
   a. The purpose of the support element is to assist staff members in analyzing and directing intelligence operations.
   b. The after-action report of the recently concluded exercise identifies several deficiencies with respect to support provided by the support element.
   c. The support element presently conducts mission-related training two days each month.
4. *Discussion.*
   a. The deficiencies in the after-action report were:
      (1) Processing of information was not accomplished in a timely manner.
      (2) Inadequate coordination among support element sections.
   b. The deficiencies noted above are interrelated and are a direct result of a training program that has been, for the most part, administratively expedient and not conducted in an environ-

ment approximating actual operational conditions. As a result, a maximum of fifteen days (average of last two years) is spent training as we would fight, with the majority of this time being taken up with personnel familiarizing themselves with the environment and establishing relationships and information channels. The problem is further aggravated by personnel turnover.

c. In the past, we have assumed that transition to a field environment would be accomplished easily. The results indicate otherwise. The basic problem is that garrison duties do not reflect field duties.

d. Two alternatives are considered feasible. These are summarized below. A detailed analysis is provided in Annex D.

(1) Increase the frequency of exercises. As a minimum, they should be conducted quarterly. The advantages of this are: more frequent training in an environment approximating actual operational conditions; smoothing out of the "peak and valley" situation that now exists; minimizing the effects of personnel turnover; and improving the level of proficiency of support personnel. The major disadvantages of this approach are that additional training time and other resources will be required.

(2) Conduct in-house training exercises. These exercises would simulate, to the extent possible, actual operating conditions.

e. Both alternatives would be in addition to the current monthly training program. This should not be discontinued, because it permits key personnel to work on specific areas of interest.

5. *Conclusions.*

a. The best solution is to have additional training exercises. This would ensure the development of a cohesive support element.

b. The second alternative, in-house training, is preferable to the current program and should be pursued should the first alternative not be approved.

6. *Recommendations.* That the conclusion in paragraph 5a be adopted.

7. *Concurrences/nonconcurrence.* List names of appropriate officers required to sign-off.

Source: Department of the Army. FM 101-5, *Staff Organization and Operations.*

# ANNEX D

# COMMANDER'S ESTIMATE OF THE SITUATION

References: Maps, charts, and other relevant documents.

1. *Mission.*

This paragraph is the commander's restated mission based on the mission analysis. It is a statement of the task(s) to be accomplished and the purpose to be achieved.

2. *The situation and course of action.*

In this paragraph, the commander considers all elements and aspects of the situation that influence operations and formulates feasible courses of action. This paragraph provides the foundation for the analysis that follows.

   a. Considerations affecting the possible courses of action. The commander determines those facts of the situation that will influence friendly and enemy actions and, therefore, may influence the choice of a course of action. The commander analyzes each fact and deduces the probable effect on other facts and on enemy and friendly actions. In the absence of facts, he uses logical assumptions.

      (1) Characteristics of the area of operations. Includes analysis of the effects of pertinent characteristics of the operations. The commander considers the following:

         (a) Weather. Analysis of predicted weather and light data for the period, together with an evaluation of the effects on friendly and enemy operations (for example, mobility) and on employment by friendly and enemy forces of means or devices affected by weather conditions, including optical and electronic line-of-sight devices and chemical, biological, and nuclear devices.

    (b) Terrain. Effect of terrain on observation and fire; cover and concealment; movement (surface and air); employment of friendly and enemy nuclear and chemical weapons and enemy biological weapons; radiating devices, such as communications, electronic warfare, and combat surveillance; unconventional warfare; psychological operations; and other aspects of military operations as appropriate. Effect of military aspects of terrain on enemy operations and own operations. Determination of key terrain features and avenues of approach.

    (c) Other pertinent factors. Analyses of political, economic, sociological, psychological, and other factors, such as hydrography, environment, communications, science, technology, material, transportation, and manpower, are gathered together with deductions about their effects on friendly and enemy operations.

(2) Enemy situation. The commander considers:

    (a) Dispositions. Locations of enemy forces, including fire support elements.

    (b) Composition. Identity, armament, and type of organization of enemy forces.

    (c) Strength. Stated in the following terms:

        (i) Committed forces. Number and size of enemy units committed against our forces.

        (ii) Reinforcements. Number and size of enemy reinforcements.

        (iii) Artillery. Number and size of supporting field artillery.

        (iv) Air and nuclear, biological, and chemical capabilities. Enemy air strength available to support ground operations; and, if known, the yield and number of nuclear warheads and quantities of chemical and biological agents and delivery means.

(v) Other considerations. Enemy forces, not listed above, known to have special capabilities, such as electronic warfare, air defense, antitank, unconventional warfare, or combat surveillance by electronic, sonic, or other means, together with deductions about their effect on combat power.

(d) Recent and present significant activities. Summaries of recent activities of the enemy that may indicate his future actions are included. If it is reasonable to believe that the enemy has knowledge of one's own situation or intentions, the commander emphasizes this fact. He pays particular attention to the pattern of employment of enemy nuclear and chemical weapons. He considers such items as enemy employment of new or unconventional weapons, and tactics or innovations in existing tactics, techniques, or materiel. He may include an evaluation of enemy intelligence collection means or techniques.

(e) Peculiarities and weaknesses. The commander indicates enemy peculiarities and weaknesses that will favorably or unfavorably influence the combat effectiveness of his forces.

(3) Own situation. The same considerations as those included in (2) above are listed for own forces. However, biological agents and delivery means are not included in the listing of considerations. The subparagraph states recent and present significant activities, peculiarities, and weaknesses and includes such items as morale, training, civil affairs, and logistics. The operations officer may compile this information for the estimate, based on knowledge of the situation and on information obtained from personnel, logistics, and civil-military operations (CMO) officers. Otherwise, the commander obtains this information directly from the personnel, operations, logistics, and CMO officers' estimates. The information is usually in abbreviated form because it may be a repetition of what is generally known. However, own dispositions are significant and must be described in sufficient detail to determine considerations that will influence the commander's choice of a course of action favorably or unfavorably,

including vulnerability to enemy nuclear, biological, or chemical attack. The information in this subparagraph of the estimate includes an indication of own vulnerability to such attack.

(4) Relative combat power. Based on an analysis of data concerning the enemy and his own situation, the commander determines and states his conclusions concerning relative combat power. These conclusions consist of an estimate of the general overall relationship of the combat power of his forces with that of the enemy forces, including significant strengths and vulnerabilities. The basic factors of combat power are maneuver units and supporting fires. Additional factors that might be considered are deception, mobility, terrain, dispositions, weather, logistic support, psychological operations, and electronic warfare. These factors do not always apply to any particular situation. For every operation, a determination of appropriate factors must be made. The commander's analysis of relative combat power provides a general background for formulating feasible courses of action and may indicate the basic nature and the characteristics of those courses of action. These conclusions assist in speeding up the estimate process by providing an indication of courses of action that would not be feasible and therefore should not be considered. The commander avoids becoming involved in an attempt to make a detailed study of personnel or weapons on both sides. He bases conclusions on a general impression of the relative capability of the two forces.

b. Enemy capabilities. Enemy capabilities are courses of action that the enemy can physically perform and that will influence the accomplishment of the mission. The intelligence officer normally identifies enemy capabilities and presents them in the intelligence estimate. If justified, the intelligence officer also provides his evaluation of the relative probability of adoption of these capabilities. The intelligence officer also must strive to inform the commander about what he believes the enemy intends to do. The commander considers all enemy capabilities presented by the intelligence officer. He may accept, revise, or discard them, or develop additional capabilities, if appropriate. The commander includes enemy vulnerabilities that are exploitable at his own higher or lower levels of command.

c. Own courses of action. A course of action is any sequence of acts which an individual or a unit may follow; a possible plan open to an individual or a commander which would accomplish or is related to the accomplishment of his mission; the scheme adopted to accomplish a job or mission; a line of conduct in an engagement. The commander may suggest that one or more courses of action be addressed when he provides guidance to the staff on the preparation of their estimates. The operations officer formulates additional courses of action that appear to be feasible. The commander considers the courses of action that the operations officer presented in his operation estimate. The commander may reject, modify, or formulate additional ones if appropriate. This procedure assists the commander in considering all significantly different courses of action. The ability to formulate feasible courses of action quickly and accurately is essential to sound decision making. The formulation and recognition of feasible courses of action depends, in part, on the perceived influence of the aspects of the situation considered in paragraph 2a and 2b of the estimate. The individual formulating courses of action should use the following criteria as a guide:

(1) Is the course of action feasible? Does the command have the capability to perform the contemplated action?

(2) Will the course of action accomplish the mission without undue damage to the command?

(3) Are the courses of action given in sufficient detail to be distinguishable, one from the other, for purposes of analysis?

Courses of action may be stated in either broad or detailed terms. During his analysis of courses of action (paragraph 3b), the estimator may add details, make revisions, and fully develop the courses of action. Each of the following elements will be included in each course of action:

(1) The type of action (attack, defend) (*what*).

(2) The time that the action will begin or be completed (when).

(3) The location of the action (in the defense, the assigned

185

sector; in the attack, the general direction of the attack) (*where*).

(4) The use of available means (*how*) (a broad indication of the maneuver elements, the form of maneuver, or the formation to be employed, and, if appropriate, nuclear and chemical fires to be employed; when necessary to distinguish between courses of action, other supporting fire may be included).

(5) The purpose of the action (*why*).

As indicated above, courses of action can be stated in broad or detailed terms. The amount of detail included is subject to the judgment of the commander; however, courses of action should include sufficient detail to be distinguishable from one another for purposes of subsequent analysis and comparison. In most instances, the distinguishing differences are in the elements of where and how. In expressing courses of action, either the *where* is used, stating only a portion of the *how* (normally used when courses of action are expressed in general terms); or the *how* is used, stating the *where* in general terms (normally used when courses of action are expressed in more detailed terms). A course of action for an offensive mission will include the *what* (attack), the *when* (time of attack), the *where* (direction of attack), the *how* (use of available means), and the *why* (purpose of the action). A course of action for a defensive mission will include the *what* (defend), the *when* (time the defense is to be effective), the *where* (may use location of forward edge of the battle area or areas units will defend), the *how* (allocation of forces to main battle area, covering force area, and reserve), and the *why* (purpose of action). Again, the amount of detail included in these elements varies according to necessity.

3. *Analysis of courses of action.*

The commander must analyze each of the courses of action formulated in paragraph 2c to determine advantages and disadvantages, to incorporate improvements, to determine requirements for supporting fire, and to define requirements for any other actions in conjunction with the course of action. This is accomplished by war gaming the course(s) of action.

The first part of the analysis (war gaming) is a preliminary analysis to identify those enemy capabilities (courses of action) listed in paragraph 2b of the estimate that will materially assist in choosing the best course of action and those that will not. Those enemy capabilities not selected for use in analysis are still valid capabilities that, if adopted by the enemy, will influence the accomplishment of the mission. However, they are of no assistance in determining the relative probability of success of own courses of action. Although these enemy capabilities are not selected, they continue to be used for reference purposes. Those enemy capabilities selected for use in analysis require judgment because there are no absolute rules governing this process. In general, when in doubt concerning the selection of a particular capability, the commander selects it. In exercising judgment, the commander:

a. Analyzes the enemy capabilities presented by the intelligence officer, paying particular attention to those capabilities having a high probability of adoption. He will probably not select a capability with a low probability of adoption.

b. Examines enemy maneuver capabilities to determine those capabilities that, if adopted, would produce a different effect on friendly courses of action. He selects these capabilities for analysis because they will assist in choosing a course of action.

c. Reexamines the selected enemy maneuver capabilities to determine the characteristics that are inherent in other capabilities. For example, the characteristics of the delay capability may be inherent in the defense capability.

d. For speed and simplicity, may combine more than one maneuver capability for analysis (for example, he may combine defense and reinforcement of the defense, or he may combine attack and reinforcement of the attack).

The second part of the analysis (war gaming) is the analysis of each of his own possible courses of action (paragraph 2c). The commander separately analyzes each friendly course of action against each of the selected enemy capabilities to determine its outcome. He visualizes the action by other sides in logical sequence from start to finish. He considers all facts of the estimate developed in paragraph 2 and their effects on the action. He determines the enemy capability to oppose the course of action and considers the degree of success in the face of enemy opposition. He weighs the degree of risk and its acceptability for each course of action. He considers active and passive measures to decrease the impact of enemy nuclear, biological or chemical, guerrilla, and air attacks. The commander makes no attempt to compare courses of action at this time. Paragraph 3 is a series of independent analyses of courses of action versus enemy capabilities. It is neither possible nor practical for the commander to reach a conclusion on the best course of action until all information developed during analysis is available and the comparison in paragraph 4 has been completed. Paragraph 3 is that part of the estimate in which the commander attempts to visualize and to anticipate all possible eventualities to discover strengths and weaknesses of each course of action. Following is an outline of one method that the commander uses to analyze an offensive course of action.

a. The commander begins by determining the combat power that the enemy has committed in the initial position that must be ruptured. He then determines the combat power required to rupture the position in the face of available enemy power.

b. The commander then visualizes the movement of units from initial positions or from positions to which units have been moved.

c. The commander visualizes the movement of units across the line of departure and the effect of enemy reaction on reinforcing or countering the attack. At this time, he considers and visualizes the unit requirement for supporting attacks. He also considers the requirement for supporting fires, use of smoke, and supporting air to rupture the initial enemy position. He visualizes critical areas and incidents and notes advantages and disadvantages. When the rupture of the initial enemy position is completed, the commander develops the composition of the main attack and required supporting attack. If the initial attack fails, he makes his decision on the composition, location, and possible employment of reserves.

d. The commander considers requirements for supporting fires; nuclear and chemical fires; and use of smoke, flame, and supporting air. He assesses the capability of the supporting attack to contribute to success by immobilizing enemy units or by preventing the use of reinforcements. He again visualizes critical areas and incidents and notes advantages and disadvantages. He considers employment of the reserve and makes a decision on its movement into more advantageous positions.

He repeats this process until the objective is secured.

e. Once the objective is secured, the commander considers requirements to consolidate, reorganize, build up, and move the reserve to the most advantageous positions. If the objective cannot be secured or the purpose of the course of action cannot be achieved, the course of action is discarded.

f. The commander repeats this process of analysis for each course of action against each of the selected enemy courses of action.

Once each course of action has been war gamed against each selected enemy capability, the commander should be certain that the following have been developed.

a. Requirements for readjustment of initial dispositions, force allocation (defense), or composition of the main and supporting attack forces (offense).

b. Requirements for combat support and combat service support and incorporation of deception and electronic warfare techniques.

c. Probable enemy reactions during each phase of the operation.

d. Probable critical areas and incidents and how success is to be achieved in each case.

e. Attrition of friendly and enemy forces during each phase of the operation.

f. Location of the commitment of following elements of the attacking force (when defending).

g. Location and composition of the reserve and its possible employment during various phases of the action.

h. Actions required in the objective area (offense).

i. Advantages and disadvantages of each course of action.

4. *Comparison courses of action.*

In this paragraph, the commander compares courses of action analyzed in paragraph 3 and reaches a conclusion on the best course of action. He uses his judgment, skill, and experience in making comparisons. Some advantages and disadvantages may be so insignificant that he may ignore them. As a result of his analysis, he determines the significance of each advantage and disadvantage in accomplishing the mission.

The commander lists the advantages and disadvantages that emerged during analysis of each course of action. He may organize this subparagraph using one of two methods. One method is to list each course of action with all advantages and disadvantages. A second method of comparison is to isolate certain significant factors (such as terrain, time, nuclear vulnerability, and own disposition) and to discuss all courses of action under each significant factor. When he uses this second method, the commander first determines decisive factors in the situation confronting him because there is no list of significant factors applicable to all situations. A simple decision table may be constructed to illustrate the comparison of courses of action. This technique is particularly useful with an unwritten estimate because it allows the commander's thoughts to be conveniently summarized. The commander states a conclusion on the course of action that offers the best prospect of success.

5. *Decision (Recommendation).*

The commander uses the course of action that offers the best probability of success as a basis for the decision. The commander's decision provides for the accomplishment of all elements of the restated mission. The commander's decision, the last step of the estimate, is a clear, concise statement of the general scheme of maneuver and supporting fires for the operation. The commander and staff will use it to develop the remainder of the tactical plan. The elements of *who, what, when, where, how,* and *why* are present in the course of action. The decision must include the element of *who* (the command itself or the appropriate elements of the command), and the commander elaborates this when he outlines his concept to the staff.

Source: Department of the Army. FM 101-5, *Staff Organization and Operations.*

# ANNEX E

# INTELLIGENCE ESTIMATE OF THE SITUATION

References: Maps, charts, or other documents.

1. *Mission.*

   The restated mission determined by the commander.

2. *The area of operation.*

   This paragraph discusses the influence of the area of operations used in arriving at conclusions. It is based on the facts and conclusions of the analysis of the area of operations, if one has been prepared. It may be a reference to an analysis of the area of operations if adequate coverage and discussion are contained therein.

   a. Weather.

      (1) Existing situation. Include light data and either a weather forecast or climatic information as appropriate. Use appendixes for graphic representations of weather factors and other detailed information.

      (2) Effect on enemy courses of action. Discuss the effects of weather on each enemy broad course of action (e.g., attack, defend) in terms of mobility and optical and electronic line of sight. Also include the effects of weather on biological and chemical agents; nuclear weapons and special methods, techniques, equipment, procedures, or forces. For example, airborne or air-mobile forces, surveillance devices, radio electronic combat, and deception. Each discussion concludes with a statement of whether the weather favors the course of action.

(3) Effect on own courses of action. Discuss in the same manner as in paragraph 2a(2) above.

b. Terrain.

(1) Existing situation. Use graphic representations developed during intelligence preparation of the battlefield, where possible. Include the information necessary for an understanding of observation and fire, cover and concealment, obstacles, key terrain features, and avenues of approach. Include effects of each of these factors, as appropriate, on nuclear fires, enemy biological and chemical agents, and any other pertinent considerations.

(2) Effect on enemy courses of action. Discuss in the same manner as for the effects of weather in paragraph 2a(2) above. For defensive courses of action, state the best defense area and the best terrain avenues of approach leading to it. For attack courses of action, state the best avenues of approach.

(3) Effect on own courses of action. Discuss in the same manner as for effects of weather in paragraph 2a(2) above.

c. Other Characteristics. Discuss pertinent sociology, politics, economics, psychology, and other factors, including science and technology, material, transportation, manpower, and hydrology. These factors are analyzed under the same headings as weather and terrain.

3. *Enemy situation.*

This paragraph gives enemy information that will permit later development of enemy capabilities and vulnerabilities and the refinement of these capabilities into a specific course of action and its relative probability of adoption.

a. Disposition. Reference may be made to overlays, enemy situation maps, or previously published documents.

b. Composition. Summary of order of battle of opposing forces and other enemy forces that can influence accomplishment of the mission. Reference may be made to previously published documents. Special mention is made of units capable of electronic warfare and other special operations as appropriate.

c. Strength. Enemy strength is listed as committed forces, reinforcements, artillery, air, nuclear weapons, chemical and biological agents, and other forces, such as electronic warfare, air defense, antitank, unconventional warfare and combat surveillance. The purpose of this listing is to develop enemy capabilities and vulnerabilities for the commander and staff to select courses of action. The unit mission, location of the enemy, enemy doctrine, and the level of command at which the estimate is being prepared are factors to be considered.

(1) Committed forces. List those enemy ground maneuver units with which imminent contact can be expected regardless of the specific friendly course of action implemented. Designation of enemy forces as committed forces depends on their disposition, location, controlling headquarters, and doctrine. The intelligence officer usually accounts for committed forces by the size of the unit used to oppose the friendly-sized unit used in his headquarters as a basis for planning operations. If there is doubt whether a unit is a committed force or a reinforcement, it is considered a reinforcement. This attributes to the enemy the maximum capability to reinforce his forces to oppose a given friendly course of action.

(2) Reinforcements. Include designation and location. Reinforcements are those enemy maneuver units that may or may not be employed against friendly forces, depending on the choice of a specific course of action and enemy plans. Reinforcements are enemy units not committed in or out of the friendly sector, but which can react to the friendly course of action, subject to time and distance considerations, to influence the accomplishment of the mission. Imminent contact is not expected. Disposition, location, level of control, or other factors considered at the time of the estimate are considered to determine which enemy forces are considered reinforcements.

(3) Artillery. List enemy artillery units, including those organic to maneuver units identified above as being committed and reinforcing. All artillery units which can be identified as being within supporting range should be enumerated as being in support of the committed force.

(4) Air. List the number of enemy aircraft by type within operational radius. Include the number of possible sorties per day by type of aircraft, if known.

(5) Nuclear weapons and chemical and biological agents.

193

Estimate the number, type, yield, and delivery means of enemy nuclear weapons and chemical and biological munitions or agents available to the enemy.

    (6) Other enemy forces. Estimates of other forces not listed above that are known to have special capabilities such as electronic warfare, air defense, antitank, unconventional warfare, or combat surveillance will be considered.

  d. Recent and present significant activities. Selected items of information are listed to provide a basis for analyses to determine relative probability of adoption of specific courses of action and enemy vulnerabilities. Enemy failure to take expected actions are listed as well as positive information.

  e. Peculiarities and weaknesses. List and briefly discuss peculiarities and weaknesses based on knowledge of enemy tactical doctrine and practices, the principles of war, the area of operations, and the enemy situation previously described and discussed. Indicate the extent to which there may be vulnerabilities and how they influence possible friendly courses of action. The items listed are grouped under pertinent headings as indicated below.

    (1) Personnel. An estimate of the enemy's strength usually is included if less than eighty percent of authorized strength. Status of morale is included, if known.

    (2) Intelligence. An estimate of enemy intelligence success, ineffectiveness, and susceptibility to deception and detection usually is included.

    (3) Operations. An estimate of the enemy's combat effectiveness usually is included if less than excellent.

    (4) Logistics. An estimate of the enemy's capability to support combat forces logistically is included if there are apparent weaknesses.

    (5) CMO operations. An estimate of the attitudes of the enemy and the civilian populace and the status of food, supply, medical facilities, and communications usually is needed.

    (6) Personalities. An estimate of the capabilities and/or weaknesses of the enemy commander and principal staff officers usually is included.

4. *Enemy capabilities.*

Based on all the previous information and analyses, develop and list enemy capabilities (for example, attack, defend, employ nuclear and chemical weapons). The listing provides a basis for determining those capabilities that the enemy can adopt as specific courses of action and their relative probability of adoption.

    a. Enumeration. State what, when, where, and strength for each capability.

    b. Analysis and discussion. This analysis and discussion provides a basis for conclusions on the adoption of enemy capabilities and their relative probability of adoption. Each capability or appropriate combination is discussed in a separate subparagraph. Consideration of enemy deception measures is included. Information and conclusions are tabulated as either supporting or rejecting the adoption of the capability. After listing all the evidence, each capability is judged from the enemy point of view to determine if the adoption of the capability is advantageous to the enemy. The judgments need not be made if the conclusion is obvious or if there is no evidence that the enemy will adopt the capability. The exception is the capability that will make the accomplishment of the friendly mission highly doubtful or impossible. This exception is to focus attention on dangerous threats.

5. *Conclusions.*

Based on all the previous information and analyses, conclusions are stated concerning the total effects of the area of operations on friendly courses of action; the courses of action available to the enemy, to include their relative probability of adoption; and the effects of the enemy vulnerabilities that can be exploited. These conditions assist in the selection of a friendly course of action.

    a. Effects of intelligence considerations on operations. Indicate whether the mission set forth in paragraph 1 above can be supported from the intelligence standpoint. Indicate which course(s) of action can best be supported from the intelligence standpoint.

    b. Effects of the area of operations on own courses of action. For attack courses of action, indicate the best avenues of approach. For defense courses of action, indicate the best defense areas and the best avenues of approach leading to and into the defense areas.

    c. Probable enemy courses of action. Courses of action are listed in order of relative probability of adoption. A listed course of action may include several subordinate courses of action that can be executed concurrently. Usually no more than two or three courses of action, in order of probability of adoption, can be justified by the available evidence.

d. Enemy vulnerabilities. List the effects of peculiarities and weaknesses that result in vulnerabilities that are exploitable at own higher or lower levels of command. The order of listing these vulnerabilities is of no significance.

Source: Department of the Army. FM 101-5, *Staff Organization and Operations*.

# LOGISTICS ESTIMATE OF THE SITUATION

References: Maps, charts, or other documents.
1. *Mission.*
The stated mission determined by the commander.
2. *The situation and considerations.*
   a. Intelligence situation. Information obtained from the intelligence officer is used. When the details are appropriate and the estimate is written, a brief summary and reference to the appropriate intelligence document, or an annex of the estimate, may be used.
   (1) Characteristics of the area of operations. Describe the general characteristics of the area of operations emphasizing specific aspects that may affect the logistical effort.
   (2) Enemy strength and dispositions.
   (3) Enemy capabilities.
      (a) Affecting the mission. Information should be general in nature.
      (b) Affecting logistic activities. Information should be detailed and oriented toward possible impact on logistic operations, including what is known about enemy air assault and airborne capabilities, tactical air, artillery, NBC (Nuclear Biological Chemical) capabilities, guerrilla operations, and stay-behind or by-pass enemy forces.

197

b. Tactical situation. Information obtained from the commander's planning guidance and from the operations officer is presented. Subparagraph should be a general and concise statement of tactical intentions.

(1) Present dispositions of major tactical elements. Include on overlay annex if appropriate.

(2) Possible courses of action. List all given courses of action. (These courses are carried forward through the remainder of the estimate.)

(3) Projected operations. If known, list projected operations and other planning factors required for coordination and integration of staff estimates.

c. Personnel situation. Include information obtained from the personnel officer on total strength, strengths of units, and factors for casualties, replacements, hospital returnees, etc.

(1) Present dispositions of personnel and administration units and installations that have an effect on the logistic situation.

(2) Projected developments within the personnel field likely to influence logistic operations.

d. Civil-military operations situation. Information obtained from the civil-military operations officer should be included.

(1) Present dispositions of civil-military operations units and installations that have an effect on the logistic situation.

(2) Projected developments within the civil-military operations field likely to influence logistic operations.

e. Logistic situation. This subparagraph should reflect the current status under appropriate subheadings. In the case of detailed information at higher levels of command, a summary may appear under the subheading with reference to an annex to the estimate. An overlay may be used to show all logistic units and installations, current and proposed. Information should include current status, capability, and any enhanced or reduced capability due to attached, detached, or supporting units.

(1) Maintenance. Provide a general statement about present capability, repair-time factors; posture of maintenance units; some reference to class VII (major end items) and IX (repair parts and components) status if there is impact on maintenance capability; status of class VII end items

(e.g., repair-parts vans, wreckers, etc.) that may impact on maintenance, etc.

(2) Supply. Provide overall status of controlling items and POL (petroleum, oils, and lubricants) allocations including pertinent comments on resupply availability, etc. Information can be provided under subheadings of classes of supply and should be listed in most meaningful measure (e.g., days of supply, total line items, equipment shortages by unit, etc.).

(3) Services. Provide present status, including capabilities and problems.

(4) Transportation. Provide status, capabilities, problems, unusual transport distances, highway and trafficability conditions (if not previously listed under characteristics of area), etc.

(5) Labor. Provide present situation, status, restrictions on use of civilians, etc.

(6) Facilities and construction.

(7) Other.

f. Assumptions. Any assumptions required as a basis for initiating planning or preparing the estimate. Assumptions are modified as a factual data when specific planning guidance becomes available.

3. *Analysis.*

Analyze all logistic factors for each subheading (paragraph 2e) for each course of action, indicating problems and deficiencies. Mathematical calculations performed to assess status of any class of supply, maintenance attrition rates, tonnage lift capacity, etc., are solely a means to obtain information for full analysis. This paragraph and any subparagraphs should contain narrative analysis statements derived from mathematical calculations and applied logic. The result of analysis for each course of action should provide both logistical and tactical impact.

a. Sufficiency of area. Determine if the area under control will be adequate for the combat service support operations. Will it be cleared of enemy units, will other units be sharing the same area (e.g., units passing through one another), will boundaries remain unchanged, etc.?

b. Material and Services.

(1) Maintenance.

    (2) Supply.
    (3) Services.
    (4) Transportation.
    (5) Labor.
    (6) Facilities.
    (7) Other.
4. *Comparison.*
  a. Evaluate logistic deficiencies and list the advantages and disadvantages with respect to the accomplishment of the mission.
  b. Discuss the advantages and disadvantages of each course of action under consideration. Include methods of overcoming deficiencies or modifications required in each course of action.
5. *Conclusions.*
  a. Indicate whether the mission stated in paragraph 1 above can be logistically supported.
  b. Indicate which course(s) of action can best be logistically supported.
  c. List the major logistic deficiencies that must be brought to the commander's attention. Include specific recommendations concerning the methods of eliminating or reducing the effect of these deficiencies.

Source: Department of the Army. FM 101-5, *Staff Organization and Operations.*

# ANNEX G

# OPERATIONS PLAN

1. *Situation.*
   a. Enemy forces. Information concerning enemy forces, such as composition, disposition, location, movement, estimated strength, identification, and capabilities will be considered. Reference to a published intelligence document, overlay, or annex may be sufficient.
   b. Friendly forces. Information concerning friendly forces, other than that covered by the operation plan (order), that may directly affect the action of subordinate commanders. This information usually is listed in order of higher, adjacent, supporting, and reinforcing units.
   c. Attachments and detachments. When not shown under "Task Organization," list here or in an annex units that are attached to or detached from the issuing headquarters, together with the time that attachments or detachments are effective.
   d. Assumptions. Include those situations/conditions that the commander believes will exist at the time the operation plan becomes an operation order.
2. *Mission.*
   A clear, concise statement of the task to be accomplished by the command and its purpose. The mission statement is derived from the commander's mission analysis. The mission is related in full, even if shown on the operation overlay. Paragraph 2 never has subparagraphs.

3. *Execution.*

    a. Concept of operation. This is a statement of the commander's visualization of the execution of an operation from start to completion—how the selected course of action is to be accomplished. It accurately provides subordinates the commander's intent in order that mission accomplishment is possible in the time available and in the absence of additional communications or further instructions. The concept clarifies the purpose of the operation and is stated in sufficient detail to ensure appropriate action by subordinates. Clarity and conciseness must prevail. The amount and detail should be sufficient to indicate what is to be accomplished by the force as a whole. If an operation overlay is used, it is referenced here.

      (1) The concept of operation may be a single paragraph, may be divided into two or more subparagraphs, or if unusually lengthy, may be prepared as an annex. The concept normally includes considerations of the close in battle as well as the deep battle and aspects of rear area protection. It should describe:

        (a) The employment of major ground and, when available, air maneuver elements in a "scheme of maneuver."

        (b) A plan of fire support or "scheme of fires" supporting the maneuver with air, artillery, and air defense fires.

        (c) Other aspects of the operation (for example, deception operations) that the commander considers appropriate to clarify the concept and to ensure unity of effort. The scheme of maneuver covers employment of major maneuver units and is derived primarily from the commander's decision. The plan of fire support complements the scheme of maneuver and stems from the commander's decision and from the staff planning.

      (2) When an operation involves two or more distinct phases, the concept of operation may be prepared in subparagraphs describing each phase.

    b. In subsequent separate lettered paragraphs, the specific tasks to be accomplished by each element of the command charged with execution of tactical missions are given. Tasks for subordinate commands that are described adequately on the opera-

202

tion overlay need not be repeated in these paragraphs. However, when time permits, tasks also may be stated here to ensure clarity. When instructions are multiple, they are itemized. If there is a priority or a sequence for accomplishment, it is stated.

4. *Service support.*

This paragraph contains a statement of the combat support service instructions and arrangements supporting the operation that are of primary interest to the units and formations being supported. It also will give the commander's direction to combat support service commanders. If lengthy, details may be included in an annex and referenced here. At higher levels of command, reference may be made to an administrative/logistics order. At lower levels of command, this paragraph or the support service annex may eliminate the need for an administrative/logistics plan or order.

5. *Command and signal.*

This paragraph contains instructions relative to command and to the operation of communications and electronic equipment (C-E). It normally has two subparagraphs: "Command" and "Signal." Command instructions may include command post (CP) locations and axis of CP displacement if not shown on an accompanying overlay. Liaison requirements, designation of alternate CP and succession of command will be entered in this subparagraph if not adequately covered in SOP.

Source: Department of the Army. FM 101-5, *Staff Organization and Operations.*

## ANNEX H

# BUSINESS PLAN

1. *Executive summary.*
   - Briefly describe the company's background, including date and state of incorporation and amount of capitalization. Discuss purposes for organizing a venture and initial products or services to be sold.
   - Describe the predecessor organization. List founding officers, directors, and major stockholders. If a limited partnership, list names of the general and limited partners.
   - Describe products or services currently being sold. Describe the uniqueness of the business. List product brand names, price ranges, and quality. Briefly compare to competition and latest state of the art.
   - Summarize the company's financial history with explanations of reasons for incurring a profit or loss.
   - Summarize market needs and demands, dollar volume of current market and projected market, methods of selling and distribution, pricing policies, production methods, packaging, advertising, and promotion.
   - List major customers and sales vulnerabilities.
   - Describe cyclical aspects of the business. Discuss government and regulatory bodies, such as the FDA and FTC, that have regulation and litigation pending that may affect the venture's future.

- Describe industry sales trends. Discuss causes for changes and how they may affect the company's business.
- Describe product R & D. Indicate product obsolescence, its potential effects on sales, and the need for a continual flow of new and updated products.
- Briefly describe patents and trademarks with expiration dates.
- Describe patents pending or patent applications in preparation, and give anticipated dates of approval. Describe trade secrets and other methods of protecting the products' uniqueness where patents are not appropriate.

2. *Management.*
   - Describe the organization, including key managers and their respective positions. Include organization chart in the appendix.
   - Capsulize work résumés with major accomplishments of key managers.
   - List schedule of current and proposed salaries and other compensations for each key manager. List stock ownership and stock option plans.
   - Summarize employment contracts between the company and officers and directors.
   - Note life insurance policies to protect investors from the loss of "indispensable" individuals.
   - Note qualifications of board of directors and degree of participation in strategy planning.
   - Discuss extent and cost of officer and director liability insurance.

3. *Product description.*
   - Describe the products or services, demonstrating their uniqueness. Description should include size, state of the art, service support, convenience, durability, function, and usages.
   - Describe patents and the protection they provide the product's uniqueness. Show a sample of a patent in the appendix.
   - Describe additional measures to protect the product's technology, such as secrecy or an accelerated marketing program.
   - Describe critical manufacturing materials and sources of supply. Discuss availability of materials, order/ship time, purchase economies and discounts, inventory shelf life, methods of inventory valuation, product special handling, and storage requirements.

- Discuss competitive products, indicating significant differences and why the company should capture a targeted market share.
- Describe pricing policies and their rationale. Describe costs of manufacturing and demonstrate the cost effectiveness of the product versus competition.
- Discuss the need for product liability insurance and its availability and cost.

4. *Product development.*
   - Describe current and proposed R & D projects and their respective chances for success. Discuss how these projects will meet changing market conditions.
   - Describe how to conduct a technological assessment that shows the evolution and extrapolation of the technology together with physical science laws and approaches that permit a breakthrough.
   - Describe R & D budget and how it was financed. Describe proposed R & D budgets and how they will be funded.
   - Show percent of current sales generated by past R & D. Project future sales to be generated from R & D projects.
   - Describe funding received or expected to be received from government agencies and other grant sources. Discuss how these funds flow into the company and their potential effects on legal rights to patent ownership. Describe how to ensure company patent ownership.
   - Describe company-owned or leased R & D facilities and equipment and list number of research employees and researchers with advanced college degrees and noted achievements.
   - List university affiliations and other outside R & D relationships. State the amount of R & D budget let or proposed to these affiliates.
   - Discuss R & D being conducted by competition and the effect it may have on the venture's future. List competitors and factors that may limit their development or service.
   - Discuss regulatory or approval requirements such as FDA and EPA before technology can be marketed.

5. *Manufacturing.*
   - Describe the manufacturing operation and current levels of production.

- Describe existing and proposed capacity for levels of production.
- Discuss production costs at different volume levels.
- Describe comparative manufacturing cost structures with competition. Describe production and operating advantages. Show technological reasons for advantages.
- Describe the plant size, location, general condition, costs, types of equipment (leased or owned), percent utilization of plant and equipment capacity, and depreciation policy.
- Describe type of operation (job shop or production line), number of employees, level of labor skills, number of shifts worked daily, union affiliations, strike history, and labor benefits.
- Describe quality control procedures, production methods, and plant layout efficiency.
- Describe average inventory turnover rates, methods of inventory valuation, availability of raw materials, backlog orders, and current status of distributors and users.
- Describe future capital expenditures for plant and equipment and how they will be financed, incremental increases in expansion costs as they relate to sales, and planned sale of assets.
- Describe subcontracted manufacturing, both current and proposed.
- Describe critical parts and whether they are sole-source.
- Discuss backup vendors and lead times.

6. *Marketing strategy.*
   - Clearly define both short- and long-term objectives.
   - Describe methods used to project dollar sales and market share objectives.
   - Forecast changing economic and market conditions and their potential effects on the company's sales and profitability.
   - Briefly describe qualitative and quantitative research analysis and how they play a critical role in making strategy decisions regarding distribution, packaging, promotion, and other marketing considerations.
   - Describe the marketplace, including size and projected growth, major customers, demographics, and major trends and characteristics.
   - Describe how the company plans to enter the marketplace or expand its market base. Discuss the use of psychographic and

demographic profiles in defining the marketplace. Describe how media support influences marketplace decisions.
- Describe the importance of a prototype of the product and its market testing prior to mass production.
- Describe competition and their respective market shares. Describe competitors' methods of distribution. Compare the product to competitors' from a marketing viewpoint.
- Discuss the feasibility and costs of entering the marketplace against existing competition. Describe the effect the product's introduction will have on the existing market. Indicate where no competition exists. Note expected future competition and intelligence regarding their funding, state of the art, marketing approach, and competitive advantages.
- Describe pricing policies and their rationale, including competitive prices, gross margin requirements, and what the market will bear.
- Discuss the buying habits of targeted customers and promotional methods on how most effectively and cost efficiently to reach them.
- Describe existing and proposed selling activities, including level of selling effort, frequency of sales and service calls, methods to identify prospective customers, and sales commission structure.
- Discuss regulatory requirements for marketing and promoting the product, such as FDA and FTC.

7. *Financial history.*
   - Capsulize balance sheets, profit-and-loss statements, and statements of sources and applications of funds for the past five years.
   - Show current reports and statements explaining material changes in conditions.
   - Describe the accounting principles used regarding depreciation, R & D, taxes, and inventories.
   - Discuss aging of accounts receivables and payables and losses because of bad debt.
   - Discuss nonrecurring items in income or expenses. Discuss unpaid taxes and existing or potential tax disputes.
   - Describe hidden or undervalued assets and liabilities contained in the balance sheet. Discuss business cycles and relate them to the company's financial needs. Show sales, costs, and profit trends and explain their reasons.

- Describe the company's capitalization, including total number of shares authorized and outstanding, voting rights, dividend payments and conversion features. List shareholders and respective number of shares owned.

8. *Financial projections.*
   - List premises and assumptions. Describe how they were developed.
   - Discuss how market research and testing were used in projecting future sales and in developing premises and assumptions.
   - Describe potential pitfalls.
   - Describe timing of account payables and receivables and show effect upon cash requirements.
   - Discuss safety margins built into pro forma statements to offset potential unexpected cost and sales shortfalls.
   - Project cash-flow statement to show sources of funds and their uses.
   - Project operating and cash-flow statements. Discuss the rationale behind projected numbers and their interrelationships with premises and assumptions.
   - Prepare a break-even analysis.

# ANNEX I

# WARNING ORDER

*Purpose.* A warning order gives subordinate units advance notice of a contemporary action or order which is to follow. Its purpose is to help units and their staffs initiate the preparations for execution of a mission by giving them the maximum warning and the essential details of impending operations including planning time available.

*Content.* The amount of detail included in a warning order depends on the time and means of communication available and the information necessary for proper planning and preparation by subordinate commanders. The warning order may include the following in sequence:

- Enemy situation, events, probable mission, task, and operation.
- Earliest time of move or degree of notice to be given to the main body.
- Rendezvous and time for assembly of an orders group, if any, stating whether commanders or representatives are to attend, and maps required; or the time at which written orders may be expected.
- Orders for preliminary action, reconnaissance, surveillance, and observation.
- Administrative and logistic instructions, any special equip-

ment required, regrouping of transport, preliminary moves to assembly areas, if necessary.

- The wording of the warning order must show clearly those parts which are executive, such as the calling of an order group, and other parts which are only a warning, such as the probable task. The recipient must not be in doubt about what he must act on and what is a warning. Usually the task (mission) of the subordinate units (other than preliminary action, reconnaissance, surveillance, and observation) should not be given in a warning order. Every warning order involving movement should state a time before which there is no move. This means that a further order must be issued before that time giving actual move timings, or extending the period before which there will be no move, or placing troops at so many hours or minutes notice to move.

*Staff activity.* A coordinating or a special staff officer may issue a warning order; however, completion of appropriate staff coordination must be assured.

*Format.* A warning order has no specified format. It is usually a brief oral or written message. The words "Warning Order" precede the message text, and an acknowledgment is usually required.

Source: Department of the Army. FM 101-5, *Staff Organization and Operations.*

# ANNEX J

# STANDING OPERATING PROCEDURES

*Purpose.* An SOP lists procedures that are unique to the organization and is used habitually for accomplishing routine or recurring actions or matters. It facilitates and expedites operations by reducing the number, length, and frequency of other types of orders; by simplifying the preparation and the transmission of other orders; by simplifying training; by promoting understanding and teamwork among the commander, staff, and troops; by advising new arrivals or newly attached units of procedures followed in the organization; and by reducing confusion and errors.

*Content.* Each command develops an SOP based on applicable portions of published procedures of higher headquarters, the desires of the commander, and the procedures that have been developed through experience. The SOP of a command includes a definite statement that the subordinate unit SOP will be based on, and conform to, that of the issuing command. The SOP is changed to meet altered conditions or practices. The SOP is sufficiently complete to advise new arrivals or newly attached units of the procedures followed in the command. The amount of detail depends on the size and state of training of the unit. Technical instructions affecting a limited number of specialists should not be included in the SOP but should be issued as separate instructions or orders, including specific SOP, as appropriate. The SOP is not to be used to consolidate actions and procedures contained in other publications and documents available to the subordinate unit.

*Staff activity.* Preparation, publication, and distribution of the command SOP are responsibilities of the operation officer. Other staff officers prepare appropriate portions of the SOP. The SOP is published in the form most effective for the command.

*Format.* Create as appropriate for specific application.

Source: Department of the Army. FM 101-5, *Staff Organization and Operations.*

# ANNEX K

# STANDING ORDERS,
# ROGER'S RANGERS

1. Don't forget nothing.
2. Have your musket clean as a whistle, hatchet scoured, sixty rounds powder and ball, and be ready to march at a minute's warning.
3. When you're on the march, act the way you would if you was sneaking up on a deer. See the enemy first.
4. Tell the truth about what you see and what you do. There is an army depending on us for correct information. You can lie all you please when you tell other folks about the Rangers. But don't never lie to a Ranger or Officer.
5. Don't never take a chance you don't have to.
6. When we're on the march we march single file, far out abreast, so it's hard to track us.
7. If we strike swamps, or soft ground, we spread out abreast, so it's hard to track us.
8. When we march, we keep moving till dark, so as to give the enemy the least possible chance at us.
9. When we camp, half the party stays awake while the other half sleeps.
10. If we take prisoners, we keep 'em separate till we have had time to examine them, so they can't cook up a story between 'em.
11. Don't ever march home the same way. Take a different route so you won't be ambushed.

12. No matter whether we travel in big parties or little ones, each party has to keep a scout twenty yards ahead, twenty yards on each flank, and twenty yards in the rear, so the main body can't be surprised and wiped out.
13. Every night you'll be told where to meet if surrounded by a superior force.
14. Don't sit down to eat without posting sentries.
15. Don't sleep beyond dawn. Dawn's when the French and Indians attack.
16. Don't cross a river by a regular ford.
17. If somebody's trailing you, make circle, come back onto your own tracks, and ambush the folks that aim to ambush you.
18. Don't stand up when the enemy's coming against you. Kneel down, lie down, hide behind a tree.
19. Let the enemy come till he's almost close enough to touch. Then let him have it and jump out and finish him up with your hatchet.

Major Robert Rogers, 1759

# BRIEFING OUTLINE

1. *Analysis of the situation.*
   a. Audience.
      (1) Size.
      (2) Nature.
          (a) Who composes the audience?
          (b) Who are the ranking members?
          (c) What are their official positions?
          (d) Where are they assigned?
          (e) How much professional knowledge of the subject do they have?
          (f) Are they generalists or specialists?
          (g) What are their interests?
          (h) What are their personal preferences?
          (i) What is the anticipated reaction?
   b. Purpose and type.
      (1) Information briefing (to perform)?
      (2) Decision briefing (to obtain decision)?
      (3) Mission briefing (to review important details)?
      (4) Staff briefing (to exchange information)?
   c. Subject.
      (1) What is the specific subject?
      (2) What is the desired coverage?
      (3) How much time will be allocated?

    d. Physical facilities.
        (1) Where will the briefing be presented?
        (2) What arrangements will be required?
        (3) What are the visual-aid facilities?
        (4) What are the deficiencies?
        (5) What actions are needed to overcome deficiencies?
2. *Schedule of Preparatory Effort.*
    a. Complete analysis of the situation.
    b. Prepare preliminary outline.
    c. Determine requirements for training aids, assistance, and recorders.
    d. Edit and/or redraft.
    e. Schedule rehearsals (facilities, critiques).
    f. Arrange for final review by responsible authority.
3. *Constructing the briefing.*
    a. Collect material.
        (1) Research.
        (2) Become familiar with subject.
        (3) Collect authoritative opinions and facts.
    b. Prepare first draft.
        (1) State problem (if necessary).
        (2) Isolate key points (facts).
        (3) Identify courses of action.
        (4) Analyze and compare courses of action. State advantages and disadvantages.
        (5) Determine conclusions and recommendations.
        (6) Prepare draft outline.
        (7) Include visual aids.
        (8) Determine appropriate authority.
        (9) Review with appropriate authority.
    c. Revise first draft and edit.
        (1) Make sure that facts are important and necessary.
        (2) Include all necessary facts.
        (3) Include answers to anticipated questions.
        (4) Refine material.
    d. Plan use of visual aids.
        (1) Check for simplicity and readability.
        (2) Develop method for use.
    e. Practice.
        (1) Rehearse (with assistants and visual aids).

    (2)  Refine.
    (3)  Isolate key points.
    (4)  Commit outline to memory.
    (5)  Develop transitions.
    (6)  Use definitive words.
4. *Follow-up.*
  a.  Ensure understanding.
  b.  Record decision.
  c.  Inform proper authorities.

Source: Department of the Army. FM 101-5, *Staff Organization and Operations.*

## ANNEX M

# PRINCIPLES OF WAR

1. *Objective.* Direct every military operation toward a clearly defined, decisive, and attainable objective.
2. *Offensive.* Seize, retain, and exploit the initiative.
3. *Mass.* Concentrate minimum essential combat power to secondary efforts.
4. *Economy of force.* Allocate minimum essential combat power to secondary efforts.
5. *Maneuver.* Place the enemy in a position of disadvantage through the flexible application of combat power.
6. *Unity of command.* For every objective, ensure unity of effort under one responsible commander.
7. *Security.* Never permit the enemy to acquire an unexpected advantage.
8. *Surprise.* Strike the enemy at a time or place or in a manner for which he is unprepared.
9. *Simplicity.* Prepare clear, uncomplicated plans and clear, concise orders to ensure thorough understanding.

Source: Department of the Army. FM 22-100, *Military Leadership.*

# ★V★

# GLOSSARY OF
# MILITARY TERMS

# GLOSSARY

Advanced Guard. The leading element of an advancing force. The primary mission to insure the uninterrupted advance of the main body. It has the following functions: a) to find and exploit gaps in the enemy's defensive system; b) to prevent the main body of the advancing force running blindly into enemy opposition; c) to clear away minor opposition or, if major opposition is met, to cover the deployment of the main body.

Agent. In intelligence usage, an organization or individual engaged in collecting and/or processing information.

Agility. Ability of friendly forces to act faster than the enemy in seizing and holding the initiative. Such greater quickness permits the rapid concentration of friendly strength against enemy vulnerabilities. This must be done rapidly so that by the time the enemy reacts to one action, another has already taken place.

Annex. A document appended to an operation order or other document to make it clearer or to give further detail.

Area of Influence. A geographical area wherein a commander is directly capable of influencing operations, by maneuver or fire support systems normally under his command or control. It is a geographical area the size of which depends upon the mission, organization, and equipment of the force involved.

Area of Interest. That area of concern to the commander, including the area of influence, areas adjacent thereto, and extending into enemy territory to the objectives of current or planned operations. This area also includes areas occupied by enemy forces who could jeopardize the accomplishment of the mission.

Assumption. A supposition on the current situation or a presupposition on the future course of events, either or both assumed to be true in the absence of positive proof, necessary to enable the commander in the process of planning to complete an estimate of the situation and make a decision on the course of action.

Base of Operations. An area or facility from which a military force begins its offensive operations, to which it falls back in case of reverse, and in which supply facilities are organized.

Chain of Command. The succession of commanding officers from a superior to a subordinate through which a command is exercised.

Command. The authority by which a commander in the military service exercises over his subordinates by virtue of rank and assignment. Command includes the authority and responsibility for effectively using available resources and for planning the employment of organizing, directing, coordinating and controlling military forces for the accomplishment of assigned missions. It also includes responsibility for health, welfare, morale, and discipline of assigned personnel.

Commander's Estimate of the Situation. A logical process of reasoning by which a commander considers all the circumstances affecting the military situation and arrives at a decision as to a course of action to be taken to accomplish the mission. A commander's estimate which considers a military situation so far in the future as to require major assumptions, is called a commander's long-range estimate of the situation.

Concept of Operations. A clear and concise statement of the line of action chosen by a commander in order to accomplish his mission.

Contingency Plan. A plan for contingencies which can reasonably be anticipated in an area of responsibility.

Consolidation of Operations. Primarily defensive operations, characterized by long duration, conducted in an assigned area of responsibility, to provide a secure area in which positive effort can be devoted to internal development.

Counterattack. Attack by part or all of a defending force against an enemy attacking force, for such specific purposes as regaining ground lost or cutting off or destroying enemy advance units, and with the general objective of denying to the enemy the attainment of his purpose in attacking. In sustained defensive operations, it is undertaken to restore the battle position and is directed at limited objectives.

Counterinsurgency. Those military, paramilitary, political, economic, psychological, and civic actions taken by a government to defeat subversive insurgency.

Counterintelligence. That phase of intelligence covering all activity devoted to destroying the effectiveness of inimical foreign intelligence activities and to the protection of information against espionage, personnel against subversion, and installations or materiel against sabotage.

Course of Action. 1) Any sequence of acts which an individual or a unit may follow. 2) A possible plan open to an individual or commander which would accomplish, or is related to the accomplishment of, his mission. 3) The scheme adopted to accomplish a job or mission. 4) A line of conduct in an engagement.

Covert Operations. Operations which are so planned and executed as to conceal the identity of or permit plausible denial by the sponsor. They differ from clandestine operations in that emphasis is placed on concealment of identity of sponsor rather than on concealment of the operation.

Decision. In an estimate of the situation, a clear and concise statement of the line of action intended to be followed by the commander as the one most favorable to the successful accomplishment of his mission.

Degree of Risk. As identified by the commander, the risk to which friendly forces may be subjected from the effects of the detonation of a nuclear weapon used in the attack of a close-in enemy target; acceptable degrees of risk under differing tactical conditions are emergency, moderate, and negligible.

Delegation of Authority. The action by which a commander assigns part of his authority commensurate with the assigned task to a subordinate commander. While ultimate responsibility cannot be relinquished, delegation of authority carries with it the imposition of a measure of responsibility. The extent of the authority delegated must be clearly stated.

Depth. The extension of operations in space, time and resources. Through the use of depth, a commander obtains the necessary space to maneuver effectively; the necessary time to plan, arrange, and execute operations; and the necessary resources to win.

Directive. 1) A military communication in which policy is established or a specific action is ordered. 2) A plan issued with a view to putting it into effect when so directed, or in the event that a stated contingency arises. 3) Broadly speaking, any communication which initiates or governs action, conduct, or procedure.

Doctrine. Fundamental principles by which the military forces guide their actions in support of objectives. It is authoritative but requires judgment in application.

Enemy Capabilities. Those courses of action of which the enemy is physically capable, and that, if adopted, will affect accomplishment of our mission. The term "capabilities" includes not only the general courses of action open to the enemy, such as attack, defense, or withdrawal, but also all the particular courses of action possible under each general course of action. "Enemy capabilities" are considered in the light of all known factors affecting military operations, including time, space, weather, terrain, and the strength and disposition of enemy forces. In strategic thinking, the capabilities of a nation represent the courses of action within the poser of the nation for accomplishing its national objectives in peace or war.

Estimate of the Situation. A logical process of reasoning by which a commander considers all the circumstances affecting the military situation and arrives at a decision as to the course of action to be taken to accomplish his mission.

Evaluation. In intelligence usage, appraisal of an item of information in terms of credibility, reliability, pertinency, and accuracy. Appraisal is accomplished at several stages within the intelligence cycle with progressively different contexts. Initial evaluations, made by case officers and report officers, are focused upon the reliability of the source and the accuracy of the information as judged by data available at or close to their operational levels. Later evaluations, by intelligence analysts, are primarily concerned with verifying accuracy of information and may, in effect, convert information into intelligence.

Exploitation. 1) Taking full advantage of success in battles and following up initial gains. 2) Taking full advantage of any information that has come to hand for tactical or strategic purposes. 3) An offensive operation that usually follows a successful attack and is designed to disorganize the enemy depth.

Feint. A show of force intended to mislead the enemy. It normally consists of a shallow, limited objective attack executed by a small portion of the total force.

226

Fix. To prevent the enemy from withdrawing any part of his force from one area for use elsewhere.

Hasty Defense. A defense normally organized while in contact with the enemy or when contact is imminent and time available for the organization is limited. It is characterized by improvement of the natural defense strength of the terrain by utilization of foxholes, emplacements, and obstacles.

Hold. In an attack, to exert sufficient pressure to prevent movement or redistribution of enemy forces.

Initiative. Setting or changing the terms of battle by action. It implies an offensive spirit in the conduct of all operations. Applied to the force as a whole, initiative requires a constant effort to force the enemy to conform to friendly force's operational purpose and tempo while retaining its own freedom of action. . . . In the attack, initiative implies never allowing the enemy to recover from the initial shock of the attack. This requires surprise in selecting the time and place of attack; concentration, speed, audacity, and violence in execution; the seeking of soft spots; flexible shifting of the main effort; and prompt transition to exploitation. . . . In defense, initiative implies quickly turning the tables on the attacker.

Intelligence. The product resulting from the collection, processing, integration, analysis, evaluation and interpretation of available information concerning foreign countries or areas, which is immediately or potentially significant to the development and execution of plans, policies, and operations.

Intelligence Estimate. The appraisal, expressed in writing or orally, of available intelligence relating to a specific situation or condition with a view to determining the courses of action open to the enemy or potential enemy and the order of probability of their adoption.

Lines of Communication. All the routes, land, water, and air, which connect an operating military force with a base of operations and along which supplies and military forces move.

Logistic Estimate of the Situation. An appraisal resulting from an orderly examination of the logistic factors influencing contemplated courses of action to provide conclusions concerning the degree and manner of that influence.

Logistics. The science of planning and carrying out the movement and maintenance of forces. In its most comprehensive sense, those aspects of military operations which deal with: a) design

227

and development, acquisition, storage, movement, distribution, maintenance, evacuation, and disposition of materiel; b) movement, evacuation, and hospitalization of personnel; c) acquisition or construction, maintenance, operation, and disposition of facilities; and d) acquisition or furnishing of services.

Management. A process of establishing and attaining objectives to carry out responsibilities. Management consists of those continuing actions of planning, organizing, directing, coordinating, controlling, and evaluating the use of men, money, materials, and facilities to accomplish missions and tasks. Management is inherent in command, but it does not include as extensive authority and responsibility as command.

Mission. The task together with the purpose, which clearly indicates the action to be taken and the reason therefor.

Objective. The physical object of the action taken, e.g., a definite tactical feature, the seizure and/or holding is essential to the commander's plan.

Operation. A military action, or the carrying out of a strategic, tactical, service, training, or administrative military mission; the process of carrying on combat, including movement, supply, attack, defense and maneuvers needed to gain the objectives of any battle or campaign.

Operation Order. A directive issued by a commander to subordinate commanders for the purpose of effecting the coordinated execution of an operation.

Operation Plan. A plan for a single or series of connected operations to be carried out simultaneously or in succession. It is usually based upon stated assumptions and is the form of directive employed by higher authority to permit subordinate commanders to prepare supporting plans and orders. The designation "plan" is usually used instead of "order" in preparing for operations well in advance. An operation plan may be put into effect at a prescribed time, or on signal, and then becomes the operation order.

Order. A communication, written, oral, or by signal, which conveys instructions from a superior to a subordinate. In a broad sense, the terms "order" and "command" are synonymous. However, an order implies discretion as to the details of execution whereas a command does not.

Organic. Assigned to and forming an essential part of a military organization.

Piecemeal Attack. Offensive action in which the various units as they become available, or wherein the timing of a planned action breaks down and the action is reduced to phases with which the enemy may deal in detail.

Reconnaissance. A mission undertaken to obtain information, by visual observation or other detection methods, information about the activities and resources of an enemy or potential enemy.

Reorganize. Restore order in a unit after combat, by replacing casualties, reassigning men if necessary, replenishing the ammunition supply, and performing whatever other action are necessary or possible in order to prepare the unit for further attack or pursuit of the enemy.

Reserve. Portion of a body of troops which is kept to the rear, or withheld from action at the beginning of an engagement, available for a decisive movement.

Responsibility. 1) The obligation to carry forward an assigned task to a successful conclusion. With responsibility goes authority to direct and take the necessary action to insure success. 2) The obligation for the proper custody, care, and safekeeping of property or funds entrusted to the possession or supervision of an individual.

Retrograde Movement. Any movement of a command to the rear, or away from the enemy. It may be forced by the enemy or may be made voluntarily. Such movement may be classified as withdrawal, retirement, or delaying action.

Secure. In an operational context, to gain possession of a position or terrain feature, with or without force, and make such disposition as will prevent, as far as possible, its destruction or loss by enemy action.

Situation. All the conditions and circumstances which effect a unit or command at any given time.

S.O.P. Standing operating procedure, or standing orders. A set of instructions covering those features of operations which lend themselves to a definite or standardized procedure without loss of effectiveness. The procedure is applicable unless ordered otherwise.

Stratagem. A trick, scheme, or device used for deceiving the enemy in war.

Strategy. The art and science of developing and using political, economic, psychological and military forces as necessary during peace and war, to afford the maximum support to policies, in order to increase the probabilities and favorable consequences of victory and to lessen the chances of defeat.

Surveillance. The systematic observation of aerospace, surface or sub-surface areas, places, persons, or things, by visual, aural, electronic, photographic, or other means.

Synchronization. The arrangement of battlefield activities in time, space and purpose to produce maximum relative combat power at the decisive point.

Tactics. The employment of units in combat.

Tactical Plan. Plan for a particular combat operation, exclusive of arrangements for supply, evacuation, maintenance or administration.

Task Force. A temporary grouping of units under one commander formed for the purpose of carrying out a specific operation or mission.

Tasking. The process of translating the allocation into orders, and passing these orders to the units involved. Each order normally contains sufficient detailed instructions to enable the executing agency to accomplish the mission successfully.

Terrain Exercise. An exercise in which a stated military situation is solved on the ground, the troops being imaginary and the solution usually being in writing.

Unconventional Warfare. A broad spectrum of military and paramilitary operations conducted in enemy-held, enemy-controlled or politically sensitive territory. Unconventional warfare includes, but is not limited to, the interrelated fields of guerrilla warfare, evasion and escape, subversion, sabotage, and other operations of a low visibility, covert or clandestine nature. These interrelated aspects of unconventional warfare may be prosecuted singly or collectively by predominantly indigenous personnel, usually supported and directed in varying degrees by (an) external source(s) during all conditions of war or peace.

War Game. A simulation, by whatever means, of a military operation involving two or more opposing forces, using rules, data, and procedures designed to depict an actual or assumed real life situation.

Warning Order. A preliminary notice of an order or an action which is to follow. It is designed to give subordinates time to make necessary plans and preparations.

Source: U.S. Department of Defense, *Dictionary of Military Terms.*

# BIBLIOGRAPHY

Ambrose, Stephen E. *Eisenhower's Generalship. Register of Graduates*, U.S. Military Academy Association of Graduates, 1991.

Benge, Eugene and John Hickey. *Morale and Motivation.* New York: Franklin Watts, 1984.

Deloitte, Haskins and Sells. "The Week in Review." 14 September 1984, vol. 84–37.

Department of the Army. October 1983. FM 22-100, *Military Leadership.*

Department of the Army. June 1990. FM 22-100, *Military Leadership.*

Department of the Army. May 1986. FM 100-5, *Operations.*

Department of the Army. May 1984. FM101-5, *Staff Organization and Operations.*

Department of the Army. May 1990. STP 21-I-MQS, *Military Qualification Standards I, Manual of Common Tasks.*

Department of the Army. January 1991. STP 21-II-MQS, *Military Qualification Standards II, Manual of Common Tasks.*

Dorland, Gilbert N. and John Van Der Wal. *The Business Idea.* New York: Van Nostrand Reinhold Company, 1978.

Naisbitt, John and Patricia Aburdene. *Megatrends 2000.* New York: William Morrow & Company, 1990.

Nye, Colonel Roger H. "Why Patton?" *West Point Library Newsletter,* March 1991.

Office of the Military Psychology and Leadership. 1969. "A Preliminary Evaluation of the Fourth Class System."

Palmer, Lt. General Dave. Letter to Gil Dorland, 25 January 1992.

Roberts, Wess. *Leadership Secrets of Attila the Hun.* New York: Warner Books, 1987.

Tactics Group—Attack Committee, U.S. Army Infantry School, Ft. Benning, Georgia. 1970. "Brigade and Battalion Operations Department."

U.S. Army Command and General Staff College, Fort Leavenworth, Kansas. 1 October 1981. *The Commander and Staff Subcourse.*

U.S. Department of Defense. *Dictionary of Military Terms.* Arco Publishing, 1988.

U.S. Military Academy, West Point, N.Y. Office of the Military, 1959. *Bugle Notes.*

U.S. Military Academy, West Point, N.Y. Office of the Military, 1989–93. *Bugle Notes.*

U.S. Military Academy, West Point, N.Y. Office of the Military, 1972–73. "The Fourth Class System."

U.S. Military Academy, West Point, N.Y. Office of the Military, 1990. "The Strategic Guidance for the U.S. Military Academy."

U.S. Military Academy, West Point, N.Y. Office of the Military, 1990. "2002—and Beyond. A Road Map to Our Third Century."

U.S. Military Academy, West Point, N.Y. Office of the Military, 1990. "United States Military Academy Goals."

U.S. Military Academy, West Point, N.Y. Office of the Military, *United States Military Academy 1990–91 Catalog.*

Woodward, Bob. *The Commanders.* London: Simon and Schuster, 1991.

Yamashita, Yoshimichi. "Japanese Executives Face Life Out of the Nest." *The Wall Street Journal,* 16 December 1991.

# INDEX

234